TOGAF® 10 Level 2

Enterprise Arch

Part 2 Exam

Scenario Questions

Scenario Strategies

Wonder Guide

Volume 1

Covers many questions, reasoning of answers

More than that, the Strategy to get all of them right

Note that TOGAF® 10 has an upgraded syllabus content that spans into the Core document - TOGAF® Standard Fundamental Content Version 10 and also into a few Series Guides that are added in the Exam Conformance list.

Thus, the knowledge base with it is broader, with a number of state-of-art topics well highlighted through the Series Guides.

We have taken care of referring to those contents from Series Guides that seem to be important for TOGAF® 10 Certification, in the questions and discussions in this Book as also in all other Books of this TOGAF® 10 Series. The Volume 2 of this Scenario Strategies Book gets more into questions related to Series Guides that align with ADM and other TOGAF® topics.

Inspirations for questions have come from various internet sources, including mock tests and sample questions. We thank all those behind this effort and appreciate their role in helping all those who want to get TOGAF® Certified.

We recommend that after understanding the strategy in approaching the Level 2 questions from this Book Series, all should also subsequently attempt the various on-line timed tests and also go through various e-Books and print books available with sample questions. These are available on a free or commercial basis.

This Book, along with the Volume 2, brings your focus unitedly into the Strategic Approach that you should take while preparing for the Level 2 Examination. The questions are incidental, but we want to emphasize that this is not yet another Question and Answer Book. This is a Book that takes you through techniques, strategies, approaches .... ; **these are important.**

Cartoon images are added to add value and for ease of reading and learning, cutting out the monotony.

Our thanks extend to public domain images from publicdomainvectors.org.

All Trademarks and TOGAF® including Boundaryless Information Flow™ are respected and is implied to have applied where applicable.

SQ 101 : Preliminary Phase

SomeCo Ltd. is an organization involved in the import and export of industrial goods. They are now looking to get the company listed in NYSE – New York Stock Exchange. Their financial experts have concluded that it is time to increase their capital by going for public equity.

The Enterprise is contemplating to deploy a good part of the fresh capital raised into the IT estate, improvising their software and hardware capabilities, which in turn will raise the level of Architectural and Business capability of the Enterprise.

The CIO has been sounded by the Top Management to take necessary action in this regard. CIO senses this as a big transformation and so has decided to set it as an Enterprise Architecture Initiative. The CIO expects a long-term roadmap to be drawn up for the emergence and continuous growth of all IT applications and facilities.

The CEO and the CIO have consulted each other on the next move in this direction. They have arrived at the following decisions :

It has to be a plan for long duration transformation. The funds deployed should result in an improvement of Business Capability along with Technical Capability. Resulting profits will be redeployed largely in IT assets and the earning and invest cycle will continue for few more years, say five years, before a review is done again.

There must be perpetual addition to value of the organization, based on Business and IT alignment. The organization must stay alive to all large-scale changes in business opportunities, market demands as also in Technical innovations. The past blunder of going into Digital Mobility too late should not be repeated.

You are stepping in as the newly appointed Chief Enterprise Architect. You have decided to use TOGAF® as the possible framework to assess and establish the Architecture Capability.

Select the best among the following options which will help you stay on track as per TOGAF® practices.

A. You will get into action by defining all that is needed for a new Enterprise Architecture. You will be on the lookout for the key drivers of the organization. You will set to do a Capability Assessment to arrive at the present level of Business Capability. This will be followed by making an assessment of present Architectural Capability. For this purpose, a study of gaps in business change maturity and approach to its resolution will be made. You will also define the Architecture Principles, the establishment of which is critical to setting the foundation for Architecture Governance. The exercise also takes you into stating and clarifying the framework to be used and the degree of tailoring it to suit the organization. The Enterprise Architecture Team is also established confirming the Governance and Support frameworks.

B. You will get into action by defining all that is needed for a new Enterprise Architecture. You will be on the lookout for the key drivers of the organization. You will set to do a Capability Assessment to arrive at the present level of Business Capability. This will be followed by making an assessment of present Architectural Capability. For this purpose, a study of gaps in business change maturity and approach to its resolution will be made. You will also define the Architecture Principles, the establishment of which is critical to setting the foundation for Architecture Governance. The exercise also takes you into stating and clarifying the framework to be used and the degree of tailoring it to suit the organization. The Enterprise Architecture Team is also established confirming the Governance and Support frameworks. The last step here will be to negotiate and draw up the development Partnership and necessary contract agreements.

C. You will get into action by defining all that is needed for a new Enterprise Architecture. You will be on the lookout for the key drivers of the organization. You will set to do a Capability Assessment to arrive at the present level of Business Capability. This will be followed by making an assessment of present Architectural Capability. For this purpose, a study of gaps in business change maturity and approach to its resolution will be made. The exercise also takes you into stating and clarifying the framework to be used and the degree of tailoring it to suit the organization. The Enterprise Architecture Team is also established confirming the Governance and Support frameworks. The last step here will be to negotiate and draw up the development Partnership and necessary contract agreements.

D. You will get into action by defining all that is needed for a new Enterprise Architecture. You will be on the lookout for the key drivers of the organization. You will set to do a Capability Assessment to arrive at the present level of Business Capability. This will be followed by making an assessment of present Architectural Capability. The Enterprise Architecture Team has also established confirming the Governance and Support frameworks. You, as an Enterprise Architect will also work on the budgetary requirement and allocation for this Architectural Team, as well as for the IT Operations Team.

Proceeding to tackle the question and getting full five marks:

As you read the question, note the following points:

Issues in focus : Expansion of capital ; Road map for big transformation; Current state of architecture is not yet known to you

Aims : Establish Architecture Capability

To do : Selecting best approach : Here it is towards preparing the organization

How should we approach this Scenario based question ?

We need to identify the portion of TOGAF® documentation (available online during Level 2 Exam) so that we can quickly go to that portion and focus only on that. Not more than half a minute to be spent on this search.

We notice that the first sentence in each of the four answers is : You will get into action by defining all that is needed for a new Enterprise Architecture. This is sufficient to guess that this question is on the Preliminary Phase of ADM.

2. Preliminary Phase

Chapter Contents: 2.1 Objectives | 2.2 Inputs | 2.3 Steps | 2.4 Outputs | 2.5 Approach

2. Preliminary Phase[1]

Here the sections in the documentation of that Phase is spanning into :

---

1. https://pubs.opengroup.org/togaf-standard/adm/chap02.html

RAMKI

Objectives

Inputs

Steps

Outputs

Approach

Definitely the four answer choices are not on Objectives of the Phase. (Questions on Objectives appear very often on Level 1 Certification). If you are appearing for the Combined Level 1 and Level 2, you must refer to our three-Part Book Series : TOGAF® 10 Level 1 Certification Preparation Wonder Guide.

The Inputs and Outputs are more of a list of items, and it is rare that a Scenario based question will come up on them. Some points appearing in answer choices may be understood better by looking at the list of (Architectural) Outputs.

Steps are kind of actions taken in the Phase. We should not think that they should be sequential, and we are allowed to take them in any order while staying within the Phase. Most of questions on ADM Phases do appear relating to the steps. We should have generally understood the Approach taken through the steps and the limited time for each question will not permit us to start reading and understanding the Approach that appears as a last section.

So, all we have to do for this question is to look at the steps from online documentation and compare them with each of the four answers.

Points in **regular bold** are positive and ones in ***italics bold*** are negative, in the following detailing. The **regular bold** portions indicate conformance with the step / point. If you see any portion shown in ***italics bold***, it is an indication that the answer has gone against the step / point or has missed it.

You can start with any of the four answers choices, or go in order of A) to D). We, right now, take a strategy of starting with two answers which our first cut feeling indicates as not the best answer. If you proceed in any other order, it is still ok. Subsequent questions follow A - B – C - D order in explaining the approach strategy behind each answer choice,.

Looking at answer choice C:

You will get into action by defining all that is needed for a new Enterprise Architecture. That is why we have opened section 2.3 of TOGAF® documentation[2]. (You better do that now, looking into it online, as a practice):

You will be on the lookout for the key drivers of the organization : Identifying key drivers **and elements in the organizational context – see this under** 2.5 Approach[3]

You will set to do a Capability Assessment to arrive at present level of Business Capability : Under 2.3.3

---

2. https://pubs.opengroup.org/togaf-standard/adm/chap02.html#tag_02_03

3. https://pubs.opengroup.org/togaf-standard/adm/chap02.html#tag_02_05

Determine existing enterprise and business capability

This will be followed by making an assessment of present Architectural Capability. For this purpose, a study of gaps in business change maturity and approach to its resolution will be made : Under 2.3.3 Define and Establish Enterprise Architecture Team and Organization

The exercise also takes you into stating and clarifying the framework to be used and the degree of tailoring it to suit the organization : Under 2.3.5 Tailor the TOGAF® Framework and, if any, Other Selected Architecture Framework(s)

The Enterprise Architecture Team is also established confirming the Governance and Support frameworks : 2.3.2 Confirm Governance and Support Frameworks

The last step here will be to negotiate and draw up the development Partnership and necessary contract agreements. This happens in Phase F and G and is also an Input to Preliminary Phase, if any prior contracts do exist. TOGAF® Certification expects you to have knowledge of all ADM Phases and answer choices like this with mix up between Phases is common

Points left out:

Very important point on Establishing Architecture Principles

Observation : Two negative points and all other positive points

Looking at answer choice D:

You will get into action by defining all that is needed for a new Enterprise Architecture. – That is why we have opened section 2.3 of TOGAF® documentation[4]. (You better do that now, looking into it online):

You will be on the lookout for the key drivers of the organization : Identifying key drivers and elements in the organizational context – see this under 2.5 Approach[5]

You will set to do a Capability Assessment to arrive at present level of Business Capability : Under 2.3.3 Determine existing enterprise and business capability

This will be followed by making an assessment of present Architectural Capability. For this purpose, a study of gaps in business change maturity and approach to its resolution will be made : Under 2.3.3 Define and Establish Enterprise Architecture Team and Organization

The Enterprise Architecture Team has also established confirming the Governance and Support frameworks : 2.3.2 Confirm Governance and Support Frameworks

You, as an Enterprise Architect will also work on the budgetary requirement and allocation for this Architectural Team, *as well as for the IT Operations Team* : 2.3.3 Assess budget requirements : Note that Enterprise Architect has

---

4. https://pubs.opengroup.org/togaf-standard/adm/chap02.html#tag_02_03

5. https://pubs.opengroup.org/togaf-standard/adm/chap02.html#tag_02_05

to come up with budget requirements for Architecture team only. Not for IT Operations Team, which is another group which is only cooperating with Architecture Team and is not part of Architecture Team. This distinction of separate roles is made clear in few places, including that in Phase F

Points left out include:

Very important point on Establishing Architecture Principles

Point on Tailoring TOGAF®

Observation : Few negative points (wrong part on budget, two major step points left out) and all other positive points

Looking at answer choice B:

You will get into action by defining all that is needed for a new Enterprise Architecture. – That is why we have opened section 2.3 of TOGAF® documentation[6]. (You better do that now, looking into it online):

You will be on the lookout for the key drivers of the organization : Identifying key drivers and elements in the organizational context – see this under 2.5 Approach[7]

You will set to do a Capability Assessment to arrive at present level of Business Capability : Under 2.3.3 Determine existing enterprise and business capability

This will be followed by making an assessment of present Architectural Capability. For this purpose, a study of gaps in business change maturity and approach to its resolution will be made : Under 2.3.3 Define and Establish Enterprise Architecture Team and Organization

You will also define the Architecture Principles, the establishment of which is critical to setting the foundation for Architecture Governance : 2.3.4 Identify and Establish Architecture Principles. This is perhaps the most important point in Preliminary Phase and should never be left out

The exercise also takes you into stating and clarifying the framework to be used and the degree of tailoring it to suit the organization : Under 2.3.5 Tailor the TOGAF® Framework and, if any, Other Selected Architecture Framework(s)

The Enterprise Architecture Team has also established confirming the Governance and Support frameworks : 2.3.2 Confirm Governance and Support Frameworks

The last step here will be to negotiate and draw up the development Partnership and necessary contract agreements. This happens in Phase F and G and is also an Input to Preliminary Phase, if any prior contracts do exist. TOGAF® Certification expects you to have knowledge of all ADM Phases and answer choices like this with mix up between Phases is common

---

6. https://pubs.opengroup.org/togaf-standard/adm/chap02.html#tag_02_03

7. https://pubs.opengroup.org/togaf-standard/adm/chap02.html#tag_02_05

Observation : One negative point and all other positive points

Looking at answer choice A:

You will get into action by defining all that is needed for a new Enterprise Architecture. – That is why we have opened section 2.3 of TOGAF® documentation[8]. (You better do that now, looking into it online) :

You will be on the lookout for the key drivers of the organization : Identifying key drivers and elements in the organizational context – see this under 2.5 Approach[9]

You will set to do a Capability Assessment to arrive at present level of Business Capability : Under 2.3.3 Determine existing enterprise and business capability

This will be followed by making an assessment of present Architectural Capability. For this purpose, a study of gaps in business change maturity and approach to its resolution will be made. See under 2.3.3 Define and Establish Enterprise Architecture Team and Organization

You will also define the Architecture Principles, the establishment of which is critical to setting the foundation for Architecture Governance : 2.3.4 Identify and Establish Architecture Principles. This is perhaps the most important point in Preliminary Phase and should never be left out

The exercise also takes you into stating and clarifying the framework to be used and the degree of tailoring it to suit the organization : Under 2.3.5 Tailor the TOGAF® Framework and, if any, Other Selected Architecture Framework(s)

The Enterprise Architecture Team has also established confirming the Governance and Support frameworks : 2.3.2 Confirm Governance and Support Frameworks

Observation : All positive points

Conclusion and Answer:

Go through all four Observations.

Best answer : A

This is the correct answer, addressing Approach and Steps of the Preliminary Phase. Refer to Chapter 2.

B : Second best answer. All points covered are ok. But defining Partnership and contract agreements is an INPUT of the Preliminary Phase.

C : Third best answer. Architecture Principles must be defined and is a major missing point. Contracts are not properly placed in right ADM Phase.

D : This is the last choice. Though a few points are positive, important two steps are left out.

---

8. https://pubs.opengroup.org/togaf-standard/adm/chap02.html#tag_02_03

9. https://pubs.opengroup.org/togaf-standard/adm/chap02.html#tag_02_05

Did you notice ? The following lines are not too relevant in arriving at the answer. At best, they may give an idea of the nature of the Enterprise, size of its organization and so on. As long as it an Enterprise needing TOGAF®, rest of the points can be ignored by you even while reading the Scenario for the first time onwards

Not so relevant points :

SomeCo Ltd. is an organization involved in the import and export of industrial goods.

They are now looking to get the company listed in NYSE – New York Stock Exchange. Their financial experts have concluded that it is time to increase their capital by going for public equity.

SQ 102 : Phase A

You are one of the Enterprise Architects of an airline that operates as a low-cost, no-frills carrier. The operations are going on for last ten years. The hub of this airline is a South Asian city. Its operations are from that hub as its base and flies to destinations within four hours of flying from there. You have observed that the destination count is 46 currently and it poised become double in a year. It covers about five International destinations currently but is planning to make that as fifteen soon.

With such a growth plan in its ambitious target line, this airline is now in the verge of taking over another smaller airline that operates only to short distance locations within the country where the above-mentioned hub lies. You, the Architect, is now entrusted with the task to suggest the best way forward with one Portfolio of few related projects moving into Architectural Vision Phase.

This presupposes that an Enterprise Architecture program has been initiated, using TOGAF® as the method and guiding framework. The CIO is the sponsor of the activity.

You have been asked to explain how you would identify and engage the stakeholders at this stage of the program. Based on TOGAF®, which of the following is the best answer ?

A. You would conduct a series of business scenarios with the stakeholders impacted by the acquisition, and determine which stakeholders are likely to block the initiative and which are likely to support it. You would identify the most relevant viewpoints and validate with the stakeholders.

B. You would focus on communications with the stakeholders at the regional carrier as effective communication of targeted information to the right stakeholders at the right time is a critical success factor for such a merger. You would develop a Communications Plan to ensure they are aware of the key features of the architecture and have the opportunity to comment.

C. You would conduct a prototype project on pilot basis, as per TOGAF®, in Phase A to demonstrate to the stakeholders the technical feasibility of the approaches that are available from your preferred suppliers. Once the stakeholders confirm the approach meets their requirements you would then complete a Statement of Work and issue an Architecture Contract to your suppliers.

D. You would identify key stakeholders across both Airlines. You would classify their positions and influence, recording the results in a stakeholder map. You would then focus on key stakeholders ensuring that you identify the most relevant viewpoints for each stakeholder and validate that their concerns are being addressed.

Proceeding to tackle the question and getting full five marks:

As you read the question, note the following points:

Issues in focus : Larger airline to acquire a smaller regional carrier

Integrate the new acquisition : Integrating IT landscape of both organizations

Moves into Phase A within the initial iteration of an ADM cycle

Aims : Ensure that the architecture is embraced across the enterprise, both in the larger and newly acquired smaller

airline

To do : Explain how you would identify and engage the stakeholders at this stage of the program

How should we approach this Scenario based question ?

We need to identify the portion of TOGAF® documentation (available online during Level 2 Exam) so that we can quickly go to that portion and focus only on that. Not more than half a minute to be spent on this.

We notice that the question is about the situation where the Phase A is taken up with a portfolio of projects. There will be stakeholders of such a project. They will from both the airlines.

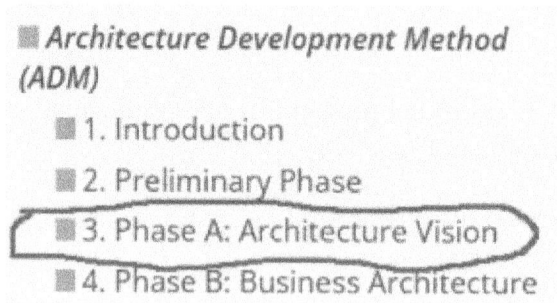

Architecture Development Method (ADM)
1. Introduction
2. Preliminary Phase
3. Phase A: Architecture Vision
4. Phase B: Business Architecture

3. Phase A: Architecture Vision[10]

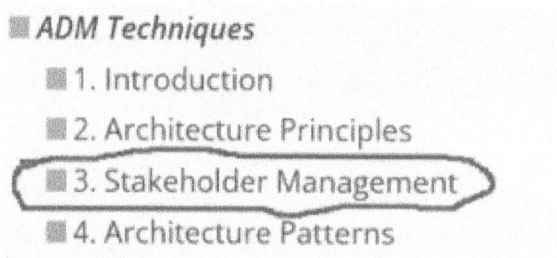

ADM Techniques
1. Introduction
2. Architecture Principles
3. Stakeholder Management
4. Architecture Patterns

3. Stakeholder Management[11]

Please decide if you need to refer to both Chapters or to just one, for this Level 2 question

We advise at this stage to also get familiar with :

6.1.1 Stakeholder Engagement and Requirements Management[12]

Which is in :

10. https://pubs.opengroup.org/togaf-standard/adm/chap03.html

11. https://pubs.opengroup.org/togaf-standard/adm-techniques/chap03.html

12. https://pubs.opengroup.org/togaf-standard/adm-practitioners/adm-practitioners_6.html#_Toc95288847

TOGAF® Series Guide
A Practitioners' Approach to Developing Enterprise
Architecture Following the TOGAF® ADM

So, all we have to do is to look at the online documentation and compare them with each of the four answers.

Points in **regular bold** are positive and ones in *italics bold* are negative, in the following detailing. The **regular bold** portions indicate conformance with the step / point. If you see any portion shown in *italics bold*, it is an indication that the answer has gone against the step / point or has missed it.

Looking at answer choice A:

Conduct a series of business scenarios with the stakeholders impacted by the acquisition : 3.3.8 Develop Architecture Vision : Business scenarios are an appropriate and useful technique to discover and document business requirements, and to articulate an Architecture Vision that responds to those requirements

Then determine which stakeholders are likely to block the initiative and which are likely to support it : 3.3.2 : Identify the key stakeholders and their concerns / objectives, and define the key business requirements to be addressed in the architecture engagement

Identify the most relevant viewpoints and validate with the stakeholders. This point is as per 3.3.2 : The concerns and viewpoints that are relevant to this project; this is captured in the Architecture Vision. However, see the point raised below:

Stakeholder Map not mentioned. This is the most important point around Phase A.

Identification of key players and the active engagement policy of Stakeholder analysis – not fully emphasized

Observation : Despite some positive points, a major negative observation seen above stands out

Looking at answer choice B:

Focus on communications with the stakeholders at the regional carrier as effective communication of targeted information to the right stakeholders at the right time is a critical success factor for such a merger. Should be done for both airlines, not just one

Develop a Communications Plan to ensure they are aware of the key features of the architecture and have the opportunity to comment. – Plan can be prepared only when shareholders of both airlines are engaged

You would finally identify the most relevant viewpoints and validate with the stakeholders. 3.3.2 : The concerns

and viewpoints that are relevant to this project; this is captured in the Architecture Vision. However, see the point raised below:

Stakeholder Map not mentioned. This is the most important point around Phase A.

Identification of key players and the active engagement policy of Stakeholder analysis – not fully emphasized

Observation : Despite one acceptable positive point, major negative observations seen above stands out

Looking at answer choice C:

You would conduct a prototype project on pilot basis, as per TOGAF®, in Phase A to demonstrate to the stakeholders the technical feasibility of the approaches that are available from your preferred suppliers. TOGAF® Phase A never mentions a pilot project

Once the stakeholders confirm the approach meets their requirements, then complete a Statement of Work and issue an Architecture Contract to your suppliers. - Contract appears in much later Phases of ADM. Suppliers are not yet selected in Phase A. We see the following only in the Objective of Phase A : Obtain approval for a Statement of Architecture Work that defines a program of works to develop and deploy the architecture outlined in the Architecture Vision

(Note : Preliminary Phase does mention about existing contracts. But project specific contracts with business users come up only from Phase E and mostly in Phase G. 2.2.2 Non-Architectural Inputs[13] to Preliminary Phase mentions ▪ Partnership and contract agreements)

Observation : Mostly absurd points are appearing here

Looking at answer choice D:

Identify key stakeholders across both Airlines : 3.3.2 Identify the key stakeholders and their concerns/objectives, and define the key business requirements to be addressed in the architecture engagement. Architectural work here onwards involves stakeholders of entire Enterprise, comprising of both airlines

Classify their positions and influence, recording the results in a stakeholder map : 3.3.2 Classify Stakeholder Positions[14] : **Develop a good understanding of the most important stakeholders and record this analysis for reference and refresh during the project.** Figure 3-2[15] **shows an example power grid. Power Grid Matrix and Stakeholder map is what is mentioned here, which is as per TOGAF®**

---

13. https://pubs.opengroup.org/togaf-standard/adm/chap02.html#tag_02_02_02

14. https://pubs.opengroup.org/togaf-standard/adm-techniques/chap03.html#tag_03_03_02

15. https://pubs.opengroup.org/togaf-standard/adm-techniques/chap03.html#tagfcjh_2

Then focus on key stakeholders ensuring that you identify the most relevant viewpoints for each stakeholder and validate that their concerns are being addressed : 3.1[16] It is essential ..... dealing with them. 3.5.2[17] Once an Architecture Vision is .... a consensus. Without this .... whole. The consensus is ... Work

Observation : All points are relevant and those points which are important towards Stakeholder Engagement at Phase A stage is covered.

Conclusion and Answer:

GO through all four Observations.

The answer will be:

Best answer : D

Stakeholder Analysis and the development of a Stakeholder Map is the technique that TOGAF® recommends for identifying and engaging the key stakeholders in Phase A. The Stakeholder Map is a major product output and used to support other outputs in this Phase, Important points in this direction is covered here

A: Second Best

This answer is less correct since it omits the Stakeholder Map approach recommended by TOGAF® to explicitly identify stakeholders. Business Scenarios are an appropriate technique to develop the Architecture Vision and can accomplish some of the engagement. This answer also lacks the identification of key players and the active engagement policy of Stakeholder analysis.

B: Third Best

This answer is less correct since it focuses on stakeholders at the regional carrier only, thus omitting key stakeholders that should be involved. The Communications Plan is produced from the work done by the Stakeholder Management approach suggested in answer A. However, the last point is ok.

C: Distracter

This answer is incorrect. TOGAF® does not recommend implementing pilot projects in Phase A to assess solution feasibility. This also is not following the recommended approach for creation and approval of a Statement of Architecture Work.

Did you notice ? A few descriptive lines in the question portion are not too relevant in arriving at the answer. Isolate them and do not spend time in reading them, expect for the purpose of understanding the area of operation and nature of the problem at hand.

---

16. https://pubs.opengroup.org/togaf-standard/adm-techniques/chap03.html#tag_03_01

17. https://pubs.opengroup.org/togaf-standard/adm/chap03.html#tag_03_05_02

SQ 103 : Requirement Management

You are having a very responsible role as the Lead Enterprise Architect in an organization which supplies electrical components including the main drive systems for the new style of electrical cars with long mileage per electrical charge. This is an upcoming greenfield industry and is expected to make waves if the gasoline prices stay high.

This company is existing only in one town of US, but has its part supplies coming from their own subsidiary company located in India. Each of these factories are having their own systems for plant operation and for production planning and scheduling. The India unit also developed customized applications without going for any COTS – Commercially Off The Shelf ERP software.

The factories and the organization as a whole are implementing lean principles in manufacturing and other spheres. Lean software development is a translation of lean manufacturing principles and practices to the software development domain. Lean offers a solid conceptual framework, values and principles, as well as good practices, derived from experience, that support agile organizations. It will result in minimized wastage and improved efficiency of all manufacturing operations.

They want you, the Lead Enterprise Architect to integrate the scheduling and other related systems with a common ERP (Enterprise Resource Planning) system with cloud enablement. Such a central cloud-based system would provide support to each of the factories and will replace, in stages, the existing systems. It would also eliminate the need for full data centers at each of the plant facilities. A reduced number of IT staff could support the remaining applications. In some cases, a third-party contractor could provide those staff or facility.

The Enterprise Architecture department under your leadership has been functioning for several years and has matured in areas of Architectural work and Architecture Governance thanks to TOGAF®.

In line with this integration need, the Architecture Board approved a Request for Architecture Work. The same was sponsored by the Chief of Manufacturing. The Architectural team to tackle the cloud-based ERP deployment is now in place. They want to examine and address concerns such as : Factory heads raising issues on forthcoming software system that will be hosted and executed at locations outside their control. Security, outage of operations and delay in effecting changes needed as per local issues are on top of the list of concerns.

Hence a meeting was convened by the Architecture Team, involving the various stakeholders and took note of all concerns like the one state above. The members of the Team now await your recommendation on the best way forward.

You will now have to select the most appropriate among the alternate suggestions that is put forward to you by the Team. The Requirement Management Phase is to take off only after you give your clear recommendation.

Based on TOGAF®, which of the following will be the best answer ?

A. The team should develop Baseline and Target Architectures for the ERPs of each of the manufacturing plants, ensuring that the views corresponding to selected viewpoints address key concerns of the stakeholders. Baseline is a list of what is available right now and Target will be in line with what ERP is needed at each decentralized plant level.

The baseline requirements should be monitored at the end of the ADM cycle when the Solution Architecture evolves as per the Target. The Requirements as per stakeholder engagement is to be identified and recorded and reviewed from time to time. The impact thereon will be studied at the later part of the ADM cycle, say towards Phase E. The

Requirement Repository however is updated at every stage.

A consolidated gap analysis between the architectures will then be used to validate the approach, and determine the capability increments needed to achieve the target state. This is what is done at the end of the ADM cycle.

B. The team should get into an exercise of vendor analysis due diligence and organize a series of meetings with supplier of ERP software, thus making a list of approved vendors and issuing the RFP (Request for Procurement)

The team should define the Architecture Vision. The team should then use that model to build consensus among the key stakeholders.

The baseline requirements should be monitored throughout the ADM cycle. No changes in Requirement is to be allowed, as the project cycles through ADM. Change Request at best is to be identified and recorded after due priority for it is assigned. The impact of proposed change is to be studied at the last Phase of ADM.

C. The team should use stakeholder analysis to understand who has concerns about the initiative.

The team should then hold a series of interviews at the level of each of the manufacturing plants using the business scenario technique. This will then enable them to identify and document the key high-level stakeholder requirements for the architecture.

The baseline requirements should be monitored throughout the ADM cycle. The changed Requirements, as the project cycles through ADM is to be identified and recorded after due priority for it is assigned. Again, important from the angle of Requirement Management. The impact thereon is to be studied at each Phase of ADM. The Requirement Repository is kept updated throughout these progressions.

D. The team should conduct a pilot project that will enable vendors on the short list to demonstrate potential solutions that will address the concerns of the stakeholders. Based on the findings of that pilot project, a complete set of retirements will be developed that will drive the evolution of the architecture.

Proceeding to tackle the question and getting full five marks:

As you read the question, note the following points:

Issues in focus : Need to minimize waste and improve the efficiency in production operations; significant reduction in process waste could be achieved by replacing the current planning and scheduling systems with a common ERP System

Focus must be on meeting the stakeholder Wishlist and on how the changes in Requirement is to be managed in the ADM cycle

Aims : Concern about the security and reliability; they expect many incremental changes would evolve as the project progresses. These concerns must be addressed

To do : Requirement Management Phase is to be followed strictly as per TOGAF®.

We need to select the approach which accommodates all the issues of the problem and allows us to proceed with the initial requirements and the takes the right path for the architecture

How should we approach this Scenario based question ?

We need to identify the portion of TOGAF® documentation (available online during Level 2 Exam) so that we can quickly go to that portion and focus only on that. Not more than half a minute to be spent on this.

Let us open Chapter 13 : ADM Architecture Requirements Management[18]

13. ADM Architecture Requirements Management

You may have to keep switching back to 3.3 : Steps of Architecture Vison, since this question deal with both and attempts to connect Stakeholder Management (Chapter 21) also with it.

3. Phase A: Architecture Vision

Chapter Contents: 3.1 Objectives | 3.2 Inputs | 3.3 Steps | 3.4 Outputs | 3.5 Approach

3. Phase A: Architecture Vision[19]

Some odd Level 2 question may require multiple places to be referred like this one, but not all questions will be like that.

All we have to do is to look at the online documentation and compare them with each of the four answers. Points in **regular bold** are positive and ones in *italics bold* are negative, in the following detailing. The **regular bold** portions indicate conformance with the step / point. If you see any portion shown in *italics bold*, it is an indication that the answer has gone against the step / point or has missed it.

Looking at answer choice A:

The team should develop Baseline and Target Architectures for the ERPs of each of the manufacturing plants, ensuring that the views corresponding to selected viewpoints address key concerns of the stakeholders. Wrong wording. Architectures in TOGAF® and as per need of this Enterprise is to be developed for the IT (software, hardware) portions as per projects and portfolios for the centralized cloud system and not for each manufacturing plant

Baseline is a list of what is available right now *and Target will be in line with what ERP is needed at each decentralized plant level.* Base line definition is correct. But Target in this question is needed for a centralized level

The baseline requirements should be monitored at the end of the ADM cycle when the Solution Architecture evolves

---

as per the Target. Actually, they are monitored throughout ADM and not at the end. Phase E will get closer to Solution Architecture, but Baseline versus Target is to be monitored in all the Phases of B to D

The Requirements as per stakeholder engagement is to be identified and recorded and reviewed from time to time. True, and comes under Requirement Management, since this Phase records them and routes them

The impact thereon will be studied at the later part of the ADM cycle, say towards Phase E. Actually, they are monitored throughout ADM and not at the end. Go and see in steps of Phases B to D and you can notice the lines; Resolve impacts across the Architecture Landscape; Conduct formal stakeholder review

The Requirement Repository however is updated at every stage. Seen in Phases B to D : Document the final mapping of the architecture within the Architecture Repository; from the selected building blocks, identify those that might be re-used (working practices, roles, business relationships, job descriptions, etc.), and publish via the Architecture Repository

A consolidated gap analysis between the architectures will then be used to validate the approach, and determine the capability increments needed to achieve the target state. This is what is done at the end of the ADM cycle. This is done in Phase E. But what happens in Phases B to D are : Perform Gap Analysis : Verify the architecture models for internal consistency and accuracy. Identify gaps between the baseline and target, using the gap analysis technique

Observation : Make note of negative points and comments thereon as appearing in above portion

Looking at answer choice B:

The team should get into an exercise of vendor analysis due diligence and organize a series of meetings with supplier of ERP software, thus making a list of approved vendors and issuing the RFP (Request for Procurement). TOGAF® does not expect EA Team to get into these issues. These are best left to the Project Management Office, Buying Department and so on. EA Team however may get to vet the technologies, preferably at Preliminary Phase with 2.3.6 Develop a Strategy and Implementation Plan for Tools and Techniques[20]. The Team will then look into such technology issues without getting into vendor specific details as ABB – Architecture Building Blocks in Phases A to D

The team should define the Architecture Vision. True. Vision Phase starts ADM Architecture cycle whenever major Change Request is accepted. 3.3.1 Establish the Architecture Project[21] is subsequently followed by 3.3.8 Develop Architecture Vision. See under 3.3.8 Develop Architecture Vision[22]: An understanding of the required artifacts will enable the stakeholders to start to scope out their decision-making which will guide subsequent phases. Based on the stakeholder concerns, business capability requirements, scope, constraints, and principles, create a high-level view of the Baseline and Target Architectures. The Architecture Vision typically covers the breadth of scope identified for the project, at a high level

The team should then use that model to build consensus among the key stakeholders. True. Stakeholder Engagement is closely related to Requirement Management. See under 13.3[23]. Sub step (Step 5) : The

20. https://pubs.opengroup.org/togaf-standard/adm/chap02.html#tag_02_03_06

21. https://pubs.opengroup.org/togaf-standard/adm/chap03.html#tag_03_03_01

22. https://pubs.opengroup.org/togaf-standard/adm/chap03.html#tag_03_03_08

23. https://pubs.opengroup.org/togaf-standard/adm/chap13.html#tag_13_03

Requirements Management Phase needs to determine stakeholder satisfaction with the decisions

The baseline requirements should be monitored throughout the ADM cycle. True. See under 13.3.[24] Sub step (Step 3) : Monitor baseline requirements. Also note: 13.5.1 General[25] : As indicated by the "Requirements Management" circle at the center of the ADM graphic, the ADM is continuously driven by the Requirements Management process

No changes in Requirement is to be allowed, as the project cycles through ADM. Not true. Some change requests are accepted at intermediate stages and a large set of changes are accepted at Phase H

Change Request at best is to be identified and recorded after due priority for it is assigned. See under 13.3.[26]. Sub step (Step 5) : Identify changed requirements and record priorities

The impact of proposed change is to be studied at the last Phase of ADM. Let us be clear. See under 13.3.[27]. Sub step (Step 7) : The architecture can be changed through its lifecycle by the Architecture, Change Management Phase (Phase H). The Requirements Management process ensures that new or changing requirements that are derived from Phase H are managed accordingly. The last point above is partly correct

Observation : A mix of positive and negative points.

 **Looking at answer choice C:**

The team should use stakeholder analysis to understand who has concerns about the initiative. Important point in this situation and in all projects. 3.3.2 Identify Stakeholders, Concerns, and Business Requirements[28]. **Also under, ADM Techniques,** 3.2 Approach to Stakeholder Management[29] : **Stakeholder analysis should be used during Phase A (Architecture Vision) to identify the key players in the engagement, and also be updated throughout each Phase; different stakeholders may be uncovered as the engagement progresses through into Opportunities & Solutions, Migration Planning, and Architecture Change Management**

The team should then hold a series of interviews at the level of each of the manufacturing plants using the business scenario technique. Mention of Business Scenario, the most appropriate technique is to be noted. See under 13.3.[30]Sub step (Step 1) : Identify/document requirements — use business scenarios, or an analogous technique

This will then enable them to identify and document the key high-level stakeholder requirements for the architecture. Important. 3.3.8 Develop Architecture Vision[31] : **Based on the stakeholder concerns, business capability requirements, scope, constraints, and principles, create a high-level view of the Baseline and Target**

---

24. https://pubs.opengroup.org/togaf-standard/adm/chap13.html#tag_13_03

25. https://pubs.opengroup.org/togaf-standard/adm/chap13.html#tag_13_05_01

26. https://pubs.opengroup.org/togaf-standard/adm/chap13.html#tag_13_03

27. https://pubs.opengroup.org/togaf-standard/adm/chap13.html#tag_13_03

28. https://pubs.opengroup.org/togaf-standard/adm/chap03.html#tag_03_03_02

29. https://pubs.opengroup.org/togaf-standard/adm-techniques/chap03.html#tag_03_02

30. https://pubs.opengroup.org/togaf-standard/adm/chap13.html#tag_13_03

31. https://pubs.opengroup.org/togaf-standard/adm/chap03.html#tag_03_03_08

Architectures. The Architecture Vision typically covers the breadth of scope identified for the project, at a high level

The baseline requirements should be monitored throughout the ADM cycle. True. See under 13.3.[32].Sub step (Step 3) : Monitor baseline requirements. Also note: 13.5.1 General[33] : As indicated by the "Requirements Management" circle at the center of the ADM graphic, the ADM is continuously driven by the Requirements Management process

The changed Requirements, as the project cycles through ADM is to be identified and recorded after due priority for it is assigned. Again, important from the angle of Requirement Management. See under 13.3.[34] Sub step (Step 5) : Identify changed requirements and record priorities

The impact thereon is to be studied at each Phase of ADM. See under 13.3.[35]. Sub step (Step 7) : The architecture can be changed through its lifecycle by the Architecture, Change Management Phase (Phase H). The Requirements Management process ensures that new or changing requirements that are derived from Phase H are managed accordingly

The Requirement Repository is kept updated throughout these progressions. Very important point for Requirement Management Phase. See under 13.3.[36].Sub step (Step 8) : Update the Architecture Requirements Repository with information relating to the changes requested, including stakeholder views affected

Observation : All positive and all relevant points covered

Looking at answer choice D:

The team should conduct a pilot project that will enable vendors on the short list to demonstrate potential solutions that will address the concerns of the stakeholders. Based on the findings of that pilot project, a complete set of retirements will be developed that will drive the evolution of the architecture. TOGAF® never suggests a pilot project. Every point in this answer choice thus is seen to be irrelevant

Observation : An answer choice that does not deserve more attention.

Conclusion and Answer:

Go through all four Observations.

The answer will be:

Best answer : C

The only answer that fits in the steps of Requirement management Phase, apart from suggesting the stakeholder analysis, business scenario and high-level stakeholder requirement document.

---

32. https://pubs.opengroup.org/togaf-standard/adm/chap13.html#tag_13_03

33. https://pubs.opengroup.org/togaf-standard/adm/chap13.html#tag_13_05_01

34. https://pubs.opengroup.org/togaf-standard/adm/chap13.html#tag_13_03

35. https://pubs.opengroup.org/togaf-standard/adm/chap13.html#tag_13_03

36. https://pubs.opengroup.org/togaf-standard/adm/chap13.html#tag_13_03

RAMKI

B : Second best answer. More positive points and less of negative points.

A : Third best answer. Some points only are relevant.

D : This is a distractor; is the worst answer for obvious reasons.

SQ 104 : Architecture Development

MegaMart is a Retail Chain which has expanded throughout India and the Far East Asia.

The Top Management has come to the decision that introducing Enterprise Architecture in streamlining and improving their overall Capability is necessary at this stage.

The CEO, under consultation with the rest of the Top Management has decided to go in for TOGAF® and adapt for the enterprise requirements. Based on the same, the organization has, by now completed the Preliminary and the Vision Phase.

It has been discovered, during the steps taken in above two Phases that the organization possesses very few architectural artifacts as of now. The Vision Phase for current portfolio of projects has also concluded that the target architecture for the project is not very clear.

As a TOGAF® Architect you will have to decide the course of action for Business Architecture and all subsequent Phases. Which of the option that you would have recommended under the circumstances described above?

A. We will mandate that the very first iteration will start with the definition of the Target Business Architecture first, in what is known as a Top down Approach among the Phases. We then will keep on iterating only in Phase B in instalments till the Target Business Architecture is refined. Then we will move on to Phase C, repeat similar process within that Phase and then move to Phase D to do the same. After Phase C and Phase D are completed this way, we iterate again to Phase B and this time get to define the baseline Business Architecture. This will be followed by our analysis of the gaps. We thus finalize the Architecture Definitions documents for Phase B and then proceed to Phase C and Phase D.

B. We will have to start with the definition of the Baseline Business Architecture in the first iteration. This means we need to pick up the exiting as-is state of the architecture, duly influenced by the Target Architecture which is clear to us by now. Define the Architecture Definition document after analyzing the impacts and reviewing with the stakeholders. Then proceed to Phase C and Phase D. In the next iteration finalize the Target Business Architecture and proceed to Phase C and Phase D.

C. In the first iteration start with the definition of the Baseline Business Architecture with hopes of using a Bottom Up approach. Define the Architecture Definition document after analyzing the impacts and reviewing with the stakeholders.

Proceed to Phase C and Phase D. In the next iteration finalize the Target Business Architecture, determine the gaps and the roadmap, and the impact and update the Architecture Definition document after analyzing the impacts and reviewing with the stakeholders. Then proceed with the iteration.

D. In the first iteration start with the definition of the Target Business Architecture using a Top Down approach. Define the Architecture Definition document after analyzing the impacts and reviewing with the stakeholders and proceed to Phase C and Phase D.

In the next iteration finalize the Baseline Business Architecture, determine the gaps and the roadmap, and the impact and update the Architecture Definition document. After analyzing the impacts and reviewing with the stakeholders.

Then proceed with the iteration.

Proceeding to tackle the question and getting full five marks:

As you read the question, note the following points:

Issues in focus : Expanded throughout India and the Far East Asia. Issues are surely expected with the expansion.

Aims : Introducing Enterprise Architecture in streamlining and improving their overall Capability

To do : Decide the course of action for Business Architecture and all subsequent Phases.

How should we approach this Scenario based question?

You need to open, in the online documentation:

2.4 Approaches to Architecture Development[1]

Applying the ADM
2. Applying Iteration to the ADM

Two approaches can be adopted within the ADM for the development of architectures :

▪ Baseline First: in this style, an assessment of the baseline landscape is used to identify problem areas and improvement opportunities. This process is most suitable when the baseline is complex, not clearly understood, or agreed upon. This approach is common where organizational units have had a high degree of autonomy.

▪ Target First: in this style, the target solution is elaborated in detail and then mapped back to the baseline, in order to identify change activity This process is suitable when a target state is agreed at a high level and where the enterprise wishes to effectively transition to the target model.

Also see and study the iteration details : 2.5.2 Iteration within an ADM Cycle[2]

Points in **regular bold** are positive and ones in *italics bold* are negative, in the following detailing. The **regular bold** portions indicate conformance with the step / point. If you see any portion shown in *italics bold*, it is an indication that the answer has gone against the step / point or has missed it.

Looking at answer choice A:

We will mandate that the very first iteration will start with the definition of the Target Business Architecture first, in what is known as a Top down Approach among the Phases. – Not possible since the situation states that target

1. https://pubs.opengroup.org/togaf-standard/applying-the-adm/chap02.html#tag_02_04
2. https://pubs.opengroup.org/togaf-standard/applying-the-adm/chap02.html#tag_02_05_02

architecture as of now is not very clear

We then will keep on iterating only in Phase B in instalments till the Target Business Architecture is refined. Then we will move on to Phase C, repeat similar process within that Phase and then move to Phase D to do the same. Suggests multiple iteration (may be with successive version numbers) in Business Architecture till target is understood. Acceptable only if the step above is proper

After Phase C and Phase D are completed this way, we iterate again to Phase B and this time get to define the baseline Business Architecture. This will be followed by our analysis of the gaps. We thus finalize the Architecture Definitions documents for Phase B and then proceed to Phase C and Phase D. It is better if the Baseline is defined in Business Architecture before proceeding to Phase C and D

Situation is that of "As such very few architectural artifacts exist and the target architecture as of now is not very clear" : This may not need a Top Down approach in every Phase

Observation : Suggestion moves us asway from the reality that : The Vision Phase for current portfolio of projects has also concluded that the target architecture for the project is not very clear

Looking at answer choice B:

We will have to start with the definition of the Baseline Business Architecture in the first iteration. This means we need to pick up the exiting as-is state of the architecture, duly influenced by the Target Architecture which is clear to us by now. Not possible since the situation states that target architecture as of now is not very clear. Idea of **starting with Business Architecture is fine** but rest in this point is not correct

Define the Architecture Definition document after analyzing the impacts and reviewing with the stakeholders. One appearing as a sub-step in Phases B to D is : Create the Architecture Definition Document. Architecture Definition document is first defined in Business Architecture Phase

Then proceed to Phase C and Phase D. Acceptable, assuming that it still does not define the Target Architecture yet

In the next iteration finalize the Target Business Architecture and proceed to Phase C and Phase D. Not acceptable

Observation : Some acceptable points are appearing amidst major not acceptable points

Looking at answer choice C:

In the first iteration start with the definition of the Baseline Business Architecture with hopes of using a Bottom Up approach. This is the only approach possible under the situation at hand. We will have to have a clear idea of Target Architecture by the earliest, if not in the first one or two iterations

Define the Architecture Definition document after analyzing the impacts and reviewing with the stakeholders.

One appearing as a sub-step in Phases B to D is : Create the Architecture Definition Document. Architecture Definition document is first defined in Business Architecture Phase

Proceed to Phase C and Phase D. In the next iteration finalize the Target Business Architecture, determine the gaps and the roadmap, and the impact and update the Architecture Definition document after analyzing the impacts and reviewing with the stakeholders. Then proceed with the iteration. Proper approach for the given situation

Observation : All points make sense in this peculiar situation here Target is not clear and ADM has to be approached to make a target architecture through successive iterations, exactly as indicated through multiple steps and iterations in : 2.2 Iteration Cycles[3]

Looking at answer choice D:

In the first iteration start with the definition of the Target Business Architecture using a Top Down approach. Not possible since the situation states that target architecture as of now is not very clear

Define the Architecture Definition document after analyzing the impacts and reviewing with the stakeholders. One appearing as a sub-step in Phases B to D is : Create the Architecture Definition Document. Architecture Definition document is first defined in Business Architecture Phase. *But what is missing is* Proceed to Phase C and Phase D after doing this

In the next iteration finalize the Baseline Business Architecture, determine the gaps and the roadmap, and the impact and update the Architecture Definition document. After analyzing the impacts and reviewing with the stakeholders. Then proceed with the iteration. Proper approach for the given situation

Observation : More acceptable points are appearing amidst some not acceptable points

Conclusion and Answer:

Go through all four Observations.

The answer will be:

Best answer : C

Between C and D this makes better meaning.

D : Second best answer. More positive points and less of negative points

B : Third best answer. Some points only are relevant

A : This is a distractor; is the worst answer for obvious reasons

---

3. https://pubs.opengroup.org/togaf-standard/applying-the-adm/chap02.html#tag_02_02

SQ 105 : Tailoring and Adapting TOGAF®

Meanwell Corporation has the idea of going for TOGAF® for their Enterprise Architecture activities.

(Details about their industry and such other statistics, which usually appear in these questions is skipped here. Such descriptions do not add much value in finding the answer, or even in understanding the question)

They approached different Consultants to find out the best way TOGAF® can be adapted to be in line with practices within the Enterprise. They have received four different suggestions from four Consultants. The Chief Enterprise Architect is expected to select one of the suggestions which will justify the move and tells how to go ahead in adapting TOGAF® to this particular Enterprise.

If you are the Chief Enterprise Architect, which will be the best option among the four that you will choose ?

A.

TOGAF® has ADM cycle which alone can be tailored and adapted for any organization. This adaptation is to be carried out even before the very first Phase of ADM is entered. This is so because Enterprise Architecture is a permanent activity and Architecture projects will use it for years.

The intention of adaptation is to change the Phases of ADM. Also, to change iterations within that. It is suggested, after studying the need of this Enterprise, that the Phases can also be compressed as A - H being compressed to just five. This adapted framework is first approved by the Architecture Governance Board before Preliminary Phase starts.

B.

TOGAF® allows for heavy degree of tailoring of vocabulary where the jargons which are used to refer to the various architecture entities itself. Possible to change the templates, artifacts which can be produced in each Phase and the way they are presented at various stages. Specific changes are possible about iterations within each Phase or moving from Phase to Phase. It is perfectly in order to change Architectural Repository structure and almost any aspect of TOGAF® that needs an adaptation.

In view of the high flexibility that is available, it is suggested that the tailoring is to start as a detailed part of Preliminary Phase.

C.

It is the ADM, Architecture Development Method that alone is allowed to be tailored as per TOGAF®. It can be made complementary to other standard management process including project management and operations management.

It is possible for adaptation for use by prime contractors for outsourcing situations.

D.

After due consultation, we can get down to tailor the Framework. We have the option to either change the definition of the general Framework with respect what is there in every cycle of development that or we can even make adjustments for specific Phases only according to its peculiarities and particularities.

The task of updating and tailoring is to be carried out throughout the first full ADM Cycle. This will allow us make changes gradually. It is possible to change the vocabulary, the templates, the principles and even the list of mandatory artifacts. Can change structure of the Architecture Repository or even for the Enterprise Continuum.

Proceeding to tackle the question and getting full five marks:

As you read the question, note the following points:

Issues in focus : TOGAF® may need Tailoring (also known as Adapting or Customizing) before it is used by this Enterprise

Aims : Consultants rarely agree with each other. Which one view is to be accepted before rejecting others?

To do : We need to select the approach which accommodates all the issues of the problem purely as indicated in the TOGAF® documentation. After all, TOGAF® suggests ways to tailor itself

How should we approach this Scenario based question ?

We need to identify the portion of TOGAF® documentation (available online during Level 2 Exam) so that we can quickly go to that portion and focus only on that. Not more than half a minute to be spent on this.

Never forget to open appropriate TOGAF® documentation, during every Reading and exercises in Level 2 :

For this question, it is :

2.3.5 Tailor the TOGAF® Framework and, if any, Other Selected Architecture Framework(s) [4]

In Preliminary phase.

As also :

3.15 Using the TOGAF® Standard with Other Frameworks[5]

Introduction and Core Concepts

In :

Let us open : 2.3.5 Tailor the TOGAF® Framework and, if any, Other Selected Architecture Framework(s)

In this step, determine what tailoring of the TOGAF® framework is required. Consider the need for:

▪ Terminology Tailoring: Architecture practitioners should use terminology that is generally understood across the enterprise. Tailoring should produce an agreed terminology set for description of architectural content. Consideration should be given to the creation of an Enterprise Glossary, to be updated throughout the architecture process.

▪ Process Tailoring: The TOGAF® ADM provides a generic process for carrying out architecture. Process tailoring provides the opportunity to remove tasks that are already carried out elsewhere in the organization, add organization-specific tasks (such as specific checkpoints), and to align the ADM processes to external process frameworks and touchpoints.

Key touch-points to be addressed would include:

---

4. https://pubs.opengroup.org/togaf-standard/adm/chap02.html#tag_02_03_05

5. https://pubs.opengroup.org/togaf-standard/introduction/chap03.html#tag_03_15

— Links to (project and service) portfolio management processes

— Links to project lifecycle

— Links to operations handover processes

— Links to operational management processes (including configuration management, change management, and service management)

— Links to procurement processes

▪ Content Tailoring: using the TOGAF® Architecture Content Framework and Enterprise Continuum as a basis, tailoring of content structure and classification approach allows adoption of third-party content frameworks and also allows for customization of the framework to support organization-specific requirements.

Note that there is a step in Preliminary Phase : <u>2.3.5 Tailor the TOGAF® Framework and, if any, Other Selected Architecture Framework(s)</u>[6]

All we have to do is to look at the point on tailoring from online documentation and compare them with each of the four answers. Points in **regular bold** are positive and ones in ***italics bold*** are negative, in the following detailing. The **regular bold** portions indicate conformance with the step / point. If you see any portion shown in ***italics bold***, it is an indication that the answer has gone against the step / point or has missed it.

Looking at answer choice A:

TOGAF® has ADM cycle which alone can be tailored and adapted for any organization. Not correct. Many parts of TOGAF® can be tailored : Content Tailoring, Terminology Tailoring and / or Process Tailoring

This adaptation is to be carried out even before the very first Phase of ADM is entered. Actually, Preliminary Phase must be doing the Tailoring and it is a Phase under ADM

This is so because Enterprise Architecture is a permanent activity and Architecture projects will use it for years. Not every important point for the situation in question, but is OK

The intention of adaptation is to change the Phases of ADM. Also, to change iterations within that. It is suggested, after studying the need of this Enterprise, that the Phases can also be compressed as A - H being compressed to just five. Fine. This five Phase reduction is one among many possibilities

This adapted framework is first approved by the Architecture Governance Board before Preliminary Phase starts. It is approved by the Board only after Preliminary Phase prepares it and submit it

Observation : Both the sequence of tailoring and order approval are mixed up. Also, what to tailor is not correctly stated.

---

6. https://pubs.opengroup.org/togaf-standard/adm/chap02.html#tag_02_03_05

Looking at answer choice B:

TOGAF® allows for heavy degree of tailoring of vocabulary where the jargons which are used to refer to the various architecture entities itself. Possible to change the templates, artifacts which can be produced in each Phase and the way they are presented at various stages. Specific changes are possible about iterations within each Phase or moving from Phase to Phase. It is perfectly in order to change Architectural Repository structure and almost any aspect of TOGAF® that needs an adaptation. In tune with Content Tailoring, Terminology Tailoring and / or Process Tailoring

In view of the high flexibility that is available, it is suggested that the tailoring is to start as a detailed part of Preliminary Phase. True. It is one of the prominent steps of this Phase

Observation : All are relevant points, covering the aspect of TOGAF® Tailoring..

Looking at answer choice C:

TOGAF® has ADM cycle which alone can be tailored and adapted for any organization. Not correct. Many parts of TOGAF® can be tailored : Content Tailoring, Terminology Tailoring and / or Process Tailoring

It can be made complementary to other standard management processes including project management and operations management. True. See 1.3 Adapting the ADM.[7] Another reason for wanting to adapt the ADM is if the TOGAF® framework is to be integrated with another enterprise framework. Also See 3.15 Using the TOGAF® Standard with Other Frameworks[8]. This architecture tailoring may include adopting elements from other architecture frameworks, or integrating TOGAF® methods with other standard frameworks or best practices, such as ITIL®, CMMI®, COBIT®, PRINCE2®, PMBOK®, and MSP®

It is possible for adaptation for use by prime contractors for outsourcing situations. True. See 1.3 Adapting the ADM.[9] : Other possible reasons for wanting to adapt the ADM include : The ADM is being mandated for use by a prime or lead contractor in an outsourcing situation, and needs to be tailored to achieve a suitable compromise between the contractor's existing practices and the contracting enterprise's requirements

Observation : Some points are correct. But one wrong assumption about what is tailor.

---

7. https://pubs.opengroup.org/togaf-standard/adm/chap01.html#tag_01_03

8. https://pubs.opengroup.org/togaf-standard/introduction/chap03.html#tag_03_15

9. https://pubs.opengroup.org/togaf-standard/adm/chap01.html#tag_01_03

Looking at answer choice D:

After due consultation, we can get down to tailor the Framework. We have the option to either change the definition of the general Framework with respect to what is there in every cycle of development that or we can even make adjustments for specific Phases only according to its peculiarities and particularities. **Correct**

The task of updating and tailoring is to be carried out throughout the first full ADM Cycle. Not correct. Tailoring is confined to Preliminary Phase only. More requests for tailoring will trigger yet another Preliminary Phase initiative, which is above the ADM cycle itself

This will allow us to make changes gradually. It is possible to change the vocabulary, the templates, the principles and even the list of mandatory artifacts. Can change the structure of the Architecture Repository or even for the Enterprise Continuum. **True**

Observation : Only the idea of when and where to carry out the tailoring is not correct

Conclusion and Answer:

Go through all four Observations.

The answer will be:

Best answer : B

It is in line with guidelines of adopting TOGAF®, as appearing in Preliminary Phase documentation and as per ADM Guidelines. Refer to section 5.3 Adapting the ADM to see the details of this answer agrees with.

D : Second best answer. Every idea of adaptation is correct. However, it suggests to do it throughput the ADM cycle, whereas it is to be done as very first thing in Primary Phases as soon as the organizational and its structure is known.

C : Third best answer. Here the adaptation ideas are correct. What is not correct is that the statement that tailoring it is confined to changes only in ADM Phases alone. Because tailoring can be for any necessary part of TOGAF®.

A : This is relatively the last choice. Preliminary Phase is the one where tailoring is to take place. This suggestion places this much before start of a one-time Preliminary Phase. The portion about Architecture governance Board itself is incorrect, since it is also set up in parallel to the Preliminary Phase.

SQ 106 : Architecture Repository

Giveall Online Digital Company is into a variety of electronic and digital lines of business. As part of a corporate-wide Lean Manufacturing initiative, the company has defined a strategic architecture to improve its ability to meet consumer demand and improve its ability to manage its supply chain.

Their strategic architecture called for the consolidation of multiple applications that have been operating for many years. A fairly good Governance system and Capability Enhancement program is in vogue for last few years. They are conscious of following stands and adhering to regulatory norms. They also believe in following Best Practices and Reference guidelines with respect to Architecture wherever and whenever available. Despite these, the Top Management felt that all information pertaining to these are not stored in a very systematic manner.

This Enterprise is aiming for every good organization of their Architecture Repository. You are the Enterprise Architect. You have to finalize now the structure of that Repository and define as to what would go where. You are keen on following it as recommended by TOGAF®.

You found out from the existing documents that there were four different recommendations given by different people who had some idea of Enterprise Architecture. Your task right now is to narrow down to the best one among them and take it up to the rest of the team make them understand all about it.

Pick one among the four possible answers

A.

Standard Library and Reference Library are produced and lie outside the Enterprise. So, these two sections should be removed from the Architecture Repository representation.

Governance Repository and Architecture Capability are the same thing which are about Architecture Governance and the way to go about doing it. Hence the Log section should also be removed and merged with the other one.

The Architecture Meta Model is nothing but something that is produced by us with respect to architecture and so this also should be merged with this section called Architecture Landscape.

B.

The Architecture Meta Model is one where you are supposed to describe the organization specific architecture framework, as adopted by the Enterprise. Hence the Architecture Meta model section provides guidelines to carry out the architectural work.

Assets prepared and in regular use by us will be a major part of the Architecture Landscape. This is because this landscape is container for architecture representation of assets which could be used within the enterprise at any particular point of time.

The Architecture Capability portion defines the processes, structures and the parameters which relate to the Governance. Skills Repository, Architectural Standards and Architecture Charter, Architectural Standards and Architecture Building Blocks will find its place here.

C.

The Architecture Meta Model is one where you are supposed to describe the organization specific architecture framework, as adopted by the Enterprise. Hence the Architecture Meta model section provides guidelines to carry out the architectural work.

Assets prepared and in regular use by us will be a major part of the Architecture Landscape. This is because this landscape is container for architecture representation of assets which could be used within the enterprise at any particular point of time.

The Architecture Capability portion defines the processes, structures and the parameters which relate to the Governance. Skills Repository, Organizational Structure and Architecture Charter will find its place here.

D.

The Architecture Meta Model is one where you are supposed to describe the organization specific architecture framework, as adopted by the Enterprise. Hence the Architecture Meta model section provides guidelines to carry out the architectural work.

Assets prepared and in regular use by us will be a major part of the Architecture Landscape. This is because this landscape is container for architecture representation of assets which could be used within the enterprise at any particular point of time.

The Architecture Capability portion defines the processes, structures and the parameters which relate to the Governance. Skills Repository, Architectural Standards and Architecture Building Blocks produced will find its place here.

Proceeding to tackle the question and getting full five marks:

As you read the question, note the following points:

Issues in focus : Top Management felt that all information pertaining to these are not stored in a very systematic manner

Aims : A fairly good Governance system and Capability Enhancement program is in vogue for last few years. They are conscious of following stands and adhering to regulatory norms. They also believe in following Best Practices and Reference guidelines with respect to Architecture wherever and whenever available. The recommendation has to fit into this expectation

To do : Four different recommendations given by different people who had some idea of Enterprise Architecture is available. Narrow down to the best one among them and take it up to the rest of the team make them understand all about it

How should we approach this Scenario based question ?

We need to identify the portion of TOGAF® documentation (available online during Level 2 Exam) so that we can quickly go to that portion and focus only on that. Not more than half a minute to be spent on this.

Let us open Chapter 7 Architecture Repository. This is because, the question is about one or more of the six parts of the Architecture Repository.

Architecture Content
7. Architecture Repository

All we have to do is to look at the points on which portion of the Repository is about what content from online documentation and compare them with each of the four answers. Points in **regular bold** are positive and ones in *italics bold* are negative, in the following detailing. The **regular bold** portions indicate conformance with the step / point. If you see any portion shown in *italics bold*, it is an indication that the answer has gone against the step / point or has missed it.

Looking at answer choice A:

Standard Library and Reference Library are produced and lie outside the Enterprise. So, these two sections should be removed from the Architecture Repository representation. These two also can lie inside as stored portion and outside as referenced portion. These two are among the six sections of the Architecture Repository

Governance Repository and Architecture Capability are same thing which are about Architecture Governance and the way to go about doing it. Hence the Log section should also be removed and merged with the other one. These two are entirely different items. Governance Repository is record of all that happened during Governance checks, while Capability section is about various enabling features of the Enterprise regarding Capability establishment

The Architecture Meta Model is nothing but something that is produced by us with respect to architecture and so this also should be merged with this section called Architecture Landscape. Yet another incorrect observation

Better read Chapter 7 Architecture Repository right now before you proceed more, if the topic is not yet clear to you

Observation : Each and every point is wrong and has been made without any knowledge of each of the six sections of Architecture Repository

Looking at answer choice B:

The Architecture Meta Model is one where you are supposed to describe the organization specific architecture framework, as adopted by the Enterprise. Hence the Architecture Meta model section provides guidelines to carry out the architectural work. True. Tailored TOGAF® is placed here. It naturally provides guidelines of TOGAF®, with tailored additions / changes where so made

Assets prepared and in regular use by us will be a major part of the Architecture Landscape. This is because this landscape is container for architecture representation of assets which could be used within the enterprise at any particular point of time. True. The Landscape contains all assets which are currently in use

The Architecture Capability portion defines the processes, structures and the parameters which relate to the Governance. Skills Repository, Architectural Standards and Architecture Charter, *Architectural Standards and Architecture Building Blocks will find its place here.* Skills Repository, Architectural Standards and Architecture Building Blocks will find their place here. Architectural Standards and Architecture Building Blocks are not part of Architecture Capability portion

Observation : Note the mix up of sub-sections of Architecture Capability portion

Looking at answer choice C:

The Architecture Meta Model is one where you are supposed to describe the organization specific architecture framework, as adopted by the Enterprise. Hence the Architecture Meta model section provides guidelines to carry out the architectural work. True. Tailored TOGAF® is placed here. It naturally provides guidelines of TOGAF®, with tailored additions / changes where so made

Assets prepared and in regular use by us will be a major part of the Architecture Landscape. This is because this landscape is container for architecture representation of assets which could be used within the enterprise at any particular point of time. True. The Landscape contains all assets which are currently in use

The Architecture Capability portion defines the processes, structures and the parameters which relate to the Governance. Skills Repository, Organizational Structure and Architecture Charter will find its place here. True. These are the actual sub-sections of this section of the Architecture Repository

Observation : Each and every point is correct and is in line with TOGAF® material

Looking at answer choice D:

The Architecture Meta Model is one where you are supposed to describe the organization specific architecture framework, as adopted by the Enterprise. Hence the Architecture Meta model section provides guidelines to carry out the architectural work. True. Tailored TOGAF® is placed here. It naturally provides guidelines of TOGAF®, with tailored additions / changes where so made

Assets prepared and in regular use by us will be a major part of the Architecture Landscape. This is because this landscape is container for architecture representation of assets which could be used within the enterprise at any particular point of time. True. The Landscape contains all assets which are currently in use

The Architecture Capability portion defines the processes, structures and the parameters which relate to the Governance. Skills Repository, Architectural Standards and *Architecture Building Blocks* produced will find its place here. Skills Repository, Architectural Standards and Architecture Building Blocks produced will find their place here. Architecture Building Blocks produced are not part of Architecture Capability portion. It belongs to Architectural Landscape

Observation : Note the mix up of sub-sections of Architecture Capability portion

Conclusion and Answer:

Go through all four Observations.

The answer will be:

Best answer : C

Every point mentioned here about Architecture Repository and its constituents are correct.

D : Second best answer.

Rest of the portion is correct. but one error noticed : Skills Repository, Architectural Standards and Architecture Building Blocks produced will find its place here. : Architecture Building Blocks produced are not part of Architecture Capability portion. It belongs to Architectural Landscape.

B : Third best answer. Rest of the portion is correct. but two errors noticed are : Skills Repository, Architectural Standards and Architecture Building Blocks will find its place here. : Architectural Standards and Architecture Building Blocks are not part of Architecture Capability portion.

A : This is a distractor; Factually incorrect arguments appear through the suggestions.

SQ 107 : BDAT Phases and Reuse

BDAT – Business, Data, Application and Technology : Maps to Phases B to D of ADM

You are the Chief Architect from a consulting organization brought into review the work to date in the Airline and to make recommendations to the CIO and the board about recommended Components to be produced by the Architecture.

Which of the following answers best describes how TOGAF® recommends as "components", based on Phase B, C and D of ADM ?

A.

Use Case Components of how SOA is implemented between any two software solutions of Airline wanting to Communicate with each other; E & R Diagram showing relationship between Classes of the projects; Hardware components as available in each aircraft; API Components of Java and Dot Net libraries. These are the appropriate, as found by you, because " An **architectural framework** like TOGAF® consists of a technical reference model, a method for architecture development and a list of component standards, specifications, products and their interrelationships which can be used to build up architectures".

B.

You have first recognized that "**Building Blocks** represents a (potentially re-usable) component of business, IT, or architectural capability". You have also realized that such Building Blocks can be : Roles, Actors, Use Case, Data Entry and Input Screens, Application Components such as Web related ones, Technology Components such as Operating systems to Application Frameworks like Java or Dot Net, and so on.

C.

You will focus only on re-usable ones only as Components. Actors are People components and so are not to be given importance here due its non-re-usable nature. Re-use based architectural components are : Architectural and Data Principles, Data models, Coding standards, Business Process components, Business rules – These are the ones to be selected by you in the list of Re-use Components.

D.

I would seek to map application components defined in the Application Architecture Phase into a set of technology components, which represent software and hardware components, available from the market or configured within the organization into technology platforms. Application Components will be selected as per Phase B, while other Components would be selected as per Phase C and D.

Proceeding to tackle the question and getting full five marks:

As you read the question, note the following points:

Aims : Review the work to date

To do : Best description of what TOGAF® recommends as "components", based on Phase B, C and D of ADM

How should we approach this Scenario based question ?

We need to identify the portion of TOGAF® documentation (available online during Level 2 Exam) so that we can quickly go to that portion and focus only on that. Not more than half a minute to be spent on this.

It is not one portion. It is about Viewpoints in different pages for Phases B, C and D.

Architecture Content

3. Architectural Artifacts

And further, you need to you your technical knowledge to a minimal extant while attempting this question.

All we have to do is to look at the steps from online documentation and compare them with each of the four answers. Points in **regular bold** are positive and ones in *italics bold* are negative, in the following detailing. The **regular bold** portions indicate conformance with the step / point. If you see any portion shown in *italics bold*, it is an indication that the answer has gone against the step / point or has missed it.

Looking at answer choice A:

Use Case Components of how SOA is implemented between any two software solutions of Airline wanting to Communicate with each other; E & R Diagram showing relationship between Classes of the projects; Hardware components as available in each aircraft; API Components of Java and Dot Net libraries. These are the appropriate, as found by you, because " An **architectural framework** like TOGAF® consists of a technical reference model, a method for architecture development and a list of component standards, specifications, products and their interrelationships which can be used to build up architectures"

Use Case Components

E & R Diagram

Hardware components of aircraft (*Not an Architectural Component*)

API Components of Java and Dot Net (These are Library Components. *Not produced in any ADM Phase; only referred to*)

TRM, ADM method, Standards for Components, specifications, products (These are Repository Components. *Not produced in any ADM Phase)*

Observation : Not at all focused answer except for the two Greens

Looking at answer choice B:

You have first recognized that "**Building Blocks** represents a (potentially re-usable) component of business, IT, or architectural capability". You have also realized that such Building Blocks can be : Roles, Actors, Use Case, Data Entry and Input Screens, Application Components such as Web related ones, Technology Components such as Operating systems to Application Frameworks like Java or Dot Net, and so on.

Building Blocks, which can be Components, can be : Roles, Actors, Use Case, Data Entry and Input Screens

Application Components such as Web related ones

Technology Components such as Operating systems to Application Frameworks like Java or Dot Net, and so on. Though produced by others, we will be configuring them and fine tuning them as per Architectural work

Note that most of these produced in Phases B to D

Observation : A good set of points, all appropriate

Looking at answer choice C:

You will focus only on re-usable ones only as Components. Actors are People components and so are not to be given importance here due its non-re-usable nature. Re-use based architectural components are : Architectural and Data Principles, Data models, Coding standards, Business Process components, Business rules – These are the ones to be selected by you in the list of Re-use Components

Focus only on re-usable ones only as Components.

Actors : Actually, re-usable in nature. Same actor will appear on more than one diagram

Re-use based architectural components are : Architectural and Data Principles, Data models, Coding standards, Business Process components, Business rules

Observation : One assumption on Actor is out of reality from re-use angle.

Looking at answer choice D:

I would seek to map application components defined in the Application Architecture Phase into a set of technology components, which represent software and hardware components, available from the market or configured within the organization into technology platforms. Application Components will be selected as per Phase B, while other

Components would be selected as per Phase C and D

Map application components into a set of technology components

Technology components represent software and hardware components

Application Components *discovered in Phase B (incorrect)*

Observation : One point quoted out of the Phase where it occurs.

Conclusion and Answer:

Go through all four Observations.

The answer will be:

Best answer : B

Most appropriate answer. This is the most complete description based on TOGAF® definition of Components, much more Components can be identified, but all the ones mentioned are correct.

D : Second best answer, though a small error in assuming that Phase B is about application components has crept in.

C : Third best answer only because it has made an unreasonable assumption that all Components are to be re-usable.

A : This is the last choice. The answer here is a mix up between artifacts and Components and factually not correct in few places.

SQ 108 : Architecture Partitioning

MakeIT Inc is a chain of convenience stores, operating as a franchise. It has over 3000 retail outlets throughout the pan Asia region. The stores operate 24 hours a day and 7 days a week and rely on point-of-sale technology to manage their inventory.

Over the years the Architectural assets of the organization has been accumulated. However, as the newly appointed Chief Enterprise Architect you sense that there is no clear partitioning of the Architecture as suggested by TOGAF®.

Since a number of Architects are operating under you, you took the route of creating a competition among them to come up with their idea of Architectural Partitioning. Finally, you find out that only one among the following descriptions given by different architects matches that of TOGAF®, which one is that?

A.

Architecture Landscape presents an architectural representation of assets in use. Architecture Landscape is thus a framework for dividing the Architecture Landscape into three levels of granularity.

Architectures are partitioned because :

Organizational unit architectures conflict with one another.

Different teams need to work on different elements of architecture at the same time and partitions allow for specific groups of architects to own and develop specific elements of the architecture.

Effective architecture re-use requires modular architecture segments that can be taken and incorporated into broader architectures and solutions.

One way of looking at partitioning of the Landscape is:

Strategic Architecture provides an organizing framework for operational and change activity and allows for direction setting at an executive level.

Segment Architecture provides an organizing framework for operational and change activity and allows for direction setting and the development of effective architecture roadmaps at a program or portfolio level.

Capability Architecture provides an organizing framework for change activity and the development of effective architecture roadmaps realizing capability increments.

B.

Architecture Landscape presents an architectural representation of assets in use. Architecture Landscape is thus a framework for dividing the Architecture Landscape into three levels of granularity.

Architectures are partitioned because different teams need to work on different elements of architecture at the same time and partitions allow for specific groups of architects to own and develop specific elements of the architecture.

One way of looking at partitioning of the Landscape is:

Strategic Architecture provides an organizing framework for operational and change activity and allows for direction setting at an executive level.

Segment Architecture provides an organizing framework for operational and change activity and allows for direction setting at Governance level.

Capability Architecture provides an organizing framework for change activity and the development of effective architecture roadmaps realizing capability increments.

C.

Architecture Landscape presents an architectural representation of assets in use. Architecture Landscape is thus a framework for dividing the Architecture Landscape into three levels of granularity.

Architectures are partitioned because:

Different teams need to work on different elements of architecture at the same time and partitions allow for specific groups of architects to own and develop specific elements of the architecture.

Effective architecture re-use requires modular architecture segments that can be taken and incorporated into broader architectures and solutions

One way of looking at partitioning of the Landscape is:

Strategic Architecture provides an organizing framework for operational and change activity and allows for direction setting at an executive level.

Segment Architecture provides an organizing framework for operational and change activity and allows for direction setting and the development of effective architecture roadmaps at a program or portfolio level.

Capability Architecture provides an organizing framework for first time activity only and the development of rigid architecture roadmaps freezing capability increments.

D.

Architecture Landscape presents an architectural representation of assets that will be prepared in future. Architecture Landscape is thus a futuristic framework for dividing the Architecture Landscape into three levels of granularity.

Architectures are partitioned because:

Different teams need to work on same elements of architecture at the same time and partitions allow for specific groups of architects to own and develop all elements of the architecture.

Effective architecture has no scope for re-use and so requires modular architecture segments that can be fixed in nature and incorporated into broader architectures and solutions

One way of looking at partitioning of the Landscape is:

Strategic Architecture provides an organizing framework for short term operational and change activity and allows for direction setting at an executive level.

Segment Architecture provides an organizing framework for strategic and long-term approach and allows for direction setting at Governance level.

Capability Architecture provides an organizing framework for first time activity only and the development of rigid architecture roadmaps freezing capability increments.

Proceeding to tackle the question and getting full five marks:

As you read the question, note the following points:

Issues in focus : Over the years the Architectural assets of the organization has been accumulated. There is no clear partitioning of the Architecture during this growth.

Aims : Took the route of creating a competition among the Architects to come up with their idea of Architectural Partitioning.

To do : Only one among the following descriptions given by different Architects matches that of TOGAF®. Which one is that?

How should we approach this Scenario based question?

We need to identify the portion of TOGAF® documentation (available online during Level 2 Exam) so that we can quickly go to that portion and focus only on that. Not more than half a minute to be spent on this.

Let us open Chapter 4 : Architecture Partitioning.[10]

Applying the ADM

4. Architecture Partitioning

All we have to do is to look at the classification of Partitions from online documentation and compare them with each of the four answers. Points in **regular bold** are positive and ones in *italics bold* are negative, in the following detailing. The **regular bold** portions indicate conformance with the step / point. If you see any portion shown in *italics bold*, it is an indication that the answer has gone against the step / point or has missed it.

Looking at answer choice A:

Architecture Landscape presents an architectural representation of assets in use. Architecture Landscape is thus

10. https://pubs.opengroup.org/togaf-standard/applying-the-adm/chap04.html

a framework for dividing the Architecture Landscape into three levels of granularity

Architectures are partitioned because:

Organizational unit architectures conflict with one another

Different teams need to work on different elements of architecture at the same time and partitions allow for specific groups of architects to own and develop specific elements of the architecture

Effective architecture re-use requires modular architecture segments that can be taken and incorporated into broader architectures and solutions

One way of looking at partitioning of the Landscape is:

> Strategic Architecture provides an organizing framework for operational and change activity and allows for direction setting at an executive level

> Segment Architecture provides an organizing framework for operational and change activity and allows for direction setting and the development of effective architecture roadmaps at a program or portfolio level

> Capability Architecture provides an organizing framework for change activity and the development of effective architecture roadmaps realizing capability increments

Observation : Every Point here is correct

 Looking at answer choice B:

Architecture Landscape presents an architectural representation of assets in use. Architecture Landscape is thus a framework for dividing the Architecture Landscape into three levels of granularity. Correct

Architectures are partitioned because different teams need to work on different elements of architecture at the same time and partitions allow for specific groups of architects to own and develop specific elements of the architecture. Correct, but more reasons are left out

Strategic Architecture provides an organizing framework for operational and change activity and allows for direction setting at an executive level. Correct

Segment Architecture provides an organizing framework for operational and change activity and allows for direction setting at Governance level. Wrong. It is at a program or portfolio level

Capability Architecture provides an organizing framework for change activity and the development of effective architecture roadmaps realizing capability increments. Correct

Observation : Mix of correct and not correct points

Looking at answer choice C:

Architecture Landscape presents an architectural representation of assets in use. Architecture Landscape is thus a framework for dividing the Architecture Landscape into three levels of granularity. Correct

Two reasons below are correct, but a ***third one is only partly correct:***

Different teams need to work on different elements of architecture at the same time and partitions allow for specific groups of architects to own and develop specific elements of the architecture

Effective architecture re-use requires modular architecture segments that can be taken and incorporated into broader architectures and solutions

> **Strategic Architecture provides an organizing framework for operational and change activity and allows for direction setting at an executive level. Correct**

> **Segment Architecture provides an organizing framework for operational and change activity and allows for direction setting and the development of effective architecture roadmaps at a program or portfolio level. Correct**

> *Capability Architecture provides an organizing framework for first time activity only and the development of rigid architecture roadmaps freezing capability increments. Wrong*

Observation : One point is not correct

Looking at answer choice D:

Architecture Landscape presents an architectural representation of assets that will be prepared in future. Wrong. It is for assets in use

Architecture Landscape is thus a futuristic framework for dividing the Architecture Lands. Different teams need to work on different elements of architecture at the same time cape into three levels of granularity. Wrong. It is a current Framework

Different teams need to work on same elements of architecture at the same time and partitions allow for specific groups of architects to own and develop all elements of the architecture. Wrong. Different teams need to work on different elements of architecture at the same time

Effective architecture has no scope for re-use and so requires modular architecture segments that can be fixed in nature and incorporated into broader architectures and solutions. Wrong. Effective architecture re-use requires modular architecture segments that can be taken and incorporated into broader architectures and solutions

All three definitions below are wrong:

Strategic Architecture provides an organizing framework for short term operational and change activity and allows for direction setting at an executive level

Segment Architecture provides an organizing framework for strategic and long-term approach and allows for direction setting at Governance level

Capability Architecture provides an organizing framework for first time activity only and the development of rigid architecture roadmaps freezing capability increments

Observation : Nothing is correct here

Conclusion and Answer:

Go through all four Observations.

The answer will be:

Best answer : A

Every point therein is correct. It is as per Chapter 36.

C : Second best answer. Two reasons left out : 1. Effective architecture re-use requires modular architecture segments that can be taken and incorporated into broader architectures and solutions. 2. Organizational unit architectures conflict with one another.

B : Third best answer. One reason left out : Organizational unit architectures conflict with one another. Further wrong definition of Capability Architecture is seen.

D : This is a distractor; Every definition here is wrong.

SQ 109 : Business Scenarios

Net Fish Ltd. is one of the biggest world suppliers of Canned Fish. This company owns the full value chain from fishing to distribution. A new ERP system is going to be introduced as part of the effort to improve the automation and standardization of the production value chain.

The CTO sponsors this activity and issues a Request for Architecture Work. The Chief Architect asks for your support to define the business requirements for architecture and the implied technical requirements.

What is the best sequence of steps to obtain the Business Scenario ?

A. You split this work in three phases (Gather, Analyze, Review) where every one of the following steps are performed. You identify, document, and rank the problem driving the scenario. Then you identify the business and technical environment of the scenario and document it in scenario models. The objectives of the business scenario should be "SMART". You then focus on identifying the human actors (and their place in the business model) and computer actors (and their place in the technology model). You document roles, responsibilities, and measures of success per actor. If necessary you then refine the scenario.

B. You start identifying, documenting, and ranking the problem driving the scenario. Then identify the business and technical environment of the scenario and document it in scenario models. The objectives of the business scenario should be "SMART". You then focus on identifying the human actors (and their place in the business model) and computer actors (and their place in the technology model). You document roles, responsibilities, and measures of success per actor. If necessary you then refine the scenario.

C. You split this work in three phases (Gather, Analyze, Review) where every one of the following steps are performed. You start identifying, documenting, and ranking the problem driving the scenario. Then you identify the business and technical environment of the scenario and document it in scenario models. You document roles, responsibilities, and measures of success per actor. If necessary you then refine the scenario.

D. You determine the readiness factors that will impact the organization, present the readiness factors using maturity model and assess the readiness factors, including determination of readiness factor ratings. Then, you assess the risks for each readiness factor and identify improvement actions to mitigate the risk.

Proceeding to tackle the question and getting full five marks:

As you read the question, note the following points:

Issues in focus :

Enterprise owns the full value chain. A new ERP system is going to be introduced as part of the effort to improve the automation and standardization of the production value chain. Request for Architecture Work – Issued.

Aim : To define the business requirements for architecture and the implied technical requirements.

To do : Best sequence of steps to obtain the Business Scenario.

How should we approach this Level 2 Scenario based question ?

We need to identify the portion of TOGAF® documentation (available online during Section 2 of the Exam) so that we can quickly go to that portion and focus only on that. Not more than half a minute to be spent on this search.

This is in TOGAF® Series Guide : Business Scenarios[11]

Points seen above are sufficient to guess that this question is on the Chapter 3 : Creating the Business Scenario. And the section : **3.1 The Overall Process**[12]

3.1 The Overall Process

Study the Figure 1: Creating a Business Scenario

As a summary, we may state that creating a business scenario involves the following :

1. Identifying, documenting, and ranking the problem driving the scenario

2. Identifying the business and technical environment of the scenario and documenting it in scenario models

3. Identifying and documenting desired objectives (the results of handling the problems successfully); get "SMART"

4. Identifying the human actors (participants) and their place in the business model

5. Identifying computer actors (computing elements) and their place in the technology model

6. Identifying and documenting roles, responsibilities, and measures of success per actor; documenting the required scripts per actor, and the results of handling the situation

7. Checking for "fitness-for-purpose" and refining only if necessary

All we have to do is to look at the points on what fits in which part of which Continuum from online documentation and compare them with each of the four answers. Points in **regular bold** are positive and ones in *italics bold* are negative, in the following detailing. The **regular bold** portions indicate conformance with the step / point. If you see any portion shown in *italics bold*, it is an indication that the answer has gone against the step / point or has missed it.

Looking at answer choice A:

We come across many positive points :

Split this work in three phases (Gather, Analyze, Review).

Identify, document, and rank the problem driving the scenario.

Identify the business and technical environment of the scenario and document it in scenario models.

---

11. https://pubs.opengroup.org/togaf-standard/business-architecture/business-scenarios.html

12. **https://pubs.opengroup.org/togaf-standard/business-architecture/business-scenarios.html#_Toc68617081**

The objectives of the business scenario should be "SMART".

Then focus on identifying the human actors (and their place in the business model) **and computer actors** (and their place in the technology model).

Document roles, responsibilities, and measures of success per actor.

If necessary you then refine the scenario.

Looking at answer choice B:

Most but one point is correct.

Start identifying, documenting, and ranking the problem driving the scenario. - *Splitting into three, missed out.*

Then identify the business and technical environment of the scenario and document it in scenario models.

The objectives of the business scenario should be "SMART".

Then focus on identifying the human actors (and their place in the business model) **and computer actors** (and their place in the technology model).

Document roles, responsibilities, and measures of success per actor.

If necessary you then refine the scenario.

Looking at answer choice C:

Split this work in three phases (Gather, Analyze, Review).

Identify, document, and rank the problem driving the scenario.

Identify the business and technical environment of the scenario and document it in scenario models.

Document roles, responsibilities, and measures of success per actor.

If necessary you then refine the scenario.

Above points are correct, *but the list of points are incomplete as compared to what is given in TOGAF® Series Guide documentation.*

Looking at answer choice D:

Determine the readiness factors that will impact the organization.

Present the readiness factors using maturity model.

Assess the readiness factors, including determination of readiness factor ratings.

Then assess the risks for each readiness factor and identify improvement actions to mitigate the risk.

All these are irrelevant to the question. Actually part of Phase A, Business Readiness Assessment.

Conclusion and Answer:

Go through all four Observations.

The answer will be:

Best answer : A

This is the most complete description of the TOGAF® approach, as per the Series Guide.

Second best answer : B : Narrow miss to the winning post.

Third best answer : C : It is incomplete.

Distractor : D : These steps are part of the Business Transformation Readiness.

SQ 110 : Architectural Governance

JustLearn inc. is an online learning company meant for e-Learning. They are running an Enterprise Architecture practice. However, the results are not particularly good. Still there are non-coherent developments and the response to the business needs is slow.

The CEO, who was the sponsor of setting up the EA practice, is disappointed and hires you as a TOGAF® consultant to review the situation.

You run some interviews and review some of the EA processes. Your conclusion is that although they have implemented the ADM process in a very proper manner, the governance around it is poor. There is simply no governance body setup. They are executing some governance processes and try to stick to the ADM, however there is no organisational body being the authority of Enterprise Architecture.

To cover this point, you tell them to setup an Architecture Board. However, this medium size company is not familiar with this and ask you for a motivation for doing this. According to TOGAF®, what would be your best answer among the choices shown?

A.

You motivate the Role : The architecture board should be established in order to cover and to oversee the architecture project implementation.

You motivate the members:

-Mainly these executive members are from the business side together with program management representatives.

-They should have a clear authority over the projects that are in scope

Try to limit the members to around 5

You motivate the Responsibilities :

-To monitoring and control the architecture contract;

-to resolve issues and conflicts in the architecture project;

-to produce implementation governance material;

-to establish and maintain the link between the business strategy and the implementation-plans for projects;

-to identify divergence from the implementation-plan;

-to enforce architecture compliance;

-to provide the basis for all decision-making with regard to the architectures;

-to support a visible escalation capability.

B.

You motivate the Role : The architecture board role is to oversee the implementation of the business strategy.

You motivate the Members :

-Therefore, this board needs to reflect the form of the organisation.

-It should typically have executive members from different business line responsibilities.

-They should have the authority within the domain that was defined for the EA capability

Try to limit the members to around 5

You motivate the Responsibilities :

-to monitoring and control the architecture contract;

-to resolve issues and conflicts, produce usable governance material;

-establish and maintain the link between the business strategy and the architecture projects;

-to identify divergence from the architecture and plan for realignment;

-to enforce architecture compliance;

-to provide the basis for all decision-making with regard to the architectures;

-to support a visible escalation capability for out-of-bounds decisions.

C.

You motivate the Role : The architecture board should be established in order to cover and oversee the architecture project implementation.

You motivate the members:

-Mainly these executive members are from the IT side together with program management representatives

-They should have a clear authority over the projects that are in scope.

Try to limit the members to around 5.

You motivate the Responsibilities :

-To monitoring and control the architecture contract

-to resolve issues and conflicts in the architecture project;

-to do the architecture compliance reviews;

-to support a visible escalation capability.

D.

You motivate the Role : The architecture board role is to oversee the implementation of the business strategy.

You define the Members :

-Therefore, this board needs to reflect the form of the organisation

-It should typically have executive members from different line responsibilities.

-They should each have the authority over their architecture domain.

-Try to limit the members to around 5.

You define the Responsibilities :

-To monitoring and control the architecture contract;

-to resolve issues and conflicts;

-to produce usable governance material;

-to establish and maintain the link between the business strategy and the architecture projects;

-to identify divergence from the architecture and plan for realignment;

-to enforce architecture compliance;

-to provide the basis for all decision-making with regard to the architectures;

-to support a visible escalation capability for out-of-bounds decisions.

Proceeding to tackle the question and getting full five marks:

As you read the question, note the following points:

Issues in focus : Governance is poor. No governance body setup

To do : Motivation in setting up an Architecture Board

How should we approach this Scenario based question?

We need to identify the portion of TOGAF® documentation (available online during Level 2 Exam) so that we can quickly go to that portion and focus only on that. Not more than half a minute to be spent on this.

Enterprise Architecture Capability and Governance
3. Architecture Governance
4. Architecture Board

See : 4.3 : Setting Up the Architecture Board[13]

Architecture Board is to oversee the implementation of the strategy. This body should be representative of all the key stakeholders in the architecture, and will typically comprise a group of executives responsible for the review and maintenance of the overall architecture.

The recommended size for an Architecture Board is ... members.

See : 4.2 Responsibilities[14]

Providing the ....

Consistency between ...

Establishing targets for ....

Flexibility of ....

— To meet ...

— To leverage ...

Enforcement of ....

Improving the ...

Ensuring that the ...

Supporting a ...

From a governance perspective, ... is also responsible fo r:

The production of

Establishing and maintaining

Identifying

All we have to do is to look at the points from online documentation and compare them with each of the four answers. Points in **regular bold** are positive and ones in *italics bold* are negative, in the following detailing. The **regular bold** portions indicate conformance with the step / point. If you see any portion shown in *italics bold*, it is an indication that the answer has gone against the step / point or has missed it.

Looking at answer choice A:

You motivate the Role : The architecture board should be established *in order to cover and to oversee the architecture*

---

13. https://pubs.opengroup.org/togaf-standard/ea-capability-and-governance/chap04.html#tag_04_03

14. https://pubs.opengroup.org/togaf-standard/ea-capability-and-governance/chap04.html#tag_04_02

project implementation : Architecture Board is to oversee the implementation of the strategy

You motivate the members : *Mainly these executive members are from the business side together with program management* representatives : This body should be representative of all the key stakeholders in the architecture

-They should have a clear authority over the projects that are in scope : They will typically comprise a group of executives responsible for the review and maintenance of the overall architecture

Try to limit the members to around 5 : Common point in all choices

You motivate the Responsibilities :

-To monitoring and control the architecture contract : Common point in all choices

-to resolve issues and conflicts in the architecture project : Common point in all choices

-to produce implementation governance material. The production of usable governance material and activities

-to establish and maintain the link between the business strategy and the implementation-plans for projects : Establishing and maintaining the link between the implementation of the architecture, the architectural strategy and objectives embodied in the enterprise architecture, and the strategic objectives of the business

-to identify divergence from the implementation-plan : Identifying divergence from the architecture and planning activities for realignment through dispensations or policy updates : Not mentioned plan for realignment. Says implementation plan

-to enforce architecture compliance;

-to provide the basis for all decision-making with regard to the architectures;

-to support a visible escalation capability.

Observation : Few correct and few wrong points

 **Looking at answer choice B :**

You motivate the Role : The architecture board role is to oversee the implementation of the business strategy.

You motivate the Members :

-Therefore this board needs to reflect the form of the organisation.

-It should typically have executive members from different business line responsibilities : This body should be representative of all the key stakeholders in the architecture

-They should have the authority within the domain that was defined for the EA capability : They will typically comprise a group of executives responsible for the review and maintenance of the overall architecture

RAMKI

Try to limit the members to around 5 : Common point in all choices

You motivate the Responsibilities :

-to monitoring and control the architecture contract : Common point in all choices

-to resolve issues and conflicts : Common point in all choices; *does not say conflicts in the architecture project*

- **produce usable governance material : The production of usable governance material and activities**

- **to establish and maintain the link between the business strategy and the implementation-plans for projects : Establishing and maintaining the link between the implementation of the architecture, the architectural strategy and objectives embodied in the enterprise architecture, and the strategic objectives of the business**

-**to identify divergence from the architecture and plan for realignment; : Identifying divergence from the architecture and planning activities for realignment through dispensations or policy updates**

-**to enforce architecture compliance;**

-**to provide the basis for all decision-making with regard to the architectures;**

-**to support a visible escalation capability for out-of-bounds decisions**

Observation : Almost every point is correct, except for a minor one

 **Looking at answer choice C:**

You motivate the Role : The architecture board should be established *in order to cover and to oversee the architecture project implementation* : Architecture Board is to oversee the implementation of the strategy

You motivate the members:

-**Mainly these executive members are from the IT side together with program management representatives** : This body should be representative of all the key stakeholders in the architecture

-They should have a clear authority over the projects that are in scope : They will typically comprise a group of executives responsible for the review and maintenance of the overall architecture

Try to limit the members to around 5 : Common point in all choices

You motivate the Responsibilities :

-To monitoring and control the architecture contract : Common point in all choices

-to resolve issues and conflicts in the architecture project : Common point in all choices

-to do the architecture compliance reviews; Does not say Enforcement of Architecture Compliance

-to support a visible escalation capability; Does not say for out-of-bounds decisions

Observation : No positive points at all

Looking at answer choice D :

You motivate the Role. The architecture board role is to oversee the implementation of the business strategy

You define the Members :

-Therefore this board needs to reflect the form of the organisation.

-It should typically have executive members from different business line responsibilities : This body should be representative of all the key stakeholders in the architecture

-They should each have the authority over their architecture domain : They will typically comprise a group of executives responsible for the review and maintenance of the overall architecture

Try to limit the members to around 5 : Common point in all choices

You define the Responsibilities :

-To monitoring and control the architecture contract : Common point in all choices

-to resolve issues and conflicts : : Common point in all choices; *does not say conflicts in the architecture project*

-to produce usable governance material : The production of usable governance material and activities

-to establish and maintain the link between the business strategy and the implementation-plans for projects :

Establishing and maintaining the link between the implementation of the architecture, the architectural strategy and objectives embodied in the enterprise architecture, and the strategic objectives of the business

-to identify divergence from the architecture and plan for realignment : Identifying divergence from the architecture and planning activities for realignment through dispensations or policy updates

-to enforce architecture compliance;

-to provide the basis for all decision-making with regard to the architectures;

-to support a visible escalation capability for out-of-bounds decisions

Observation : Few deviations and other points covered

Conclusion and Answer:

Go through all four Observations.

The answer will be:

Best answer : B

Almost every point therein is correct and is complete. No other answer choice is better than this.

D : Second best answer.

Only a few deviations

A : Third best answer.

C : This is a distractor; Every point is wrong.

SQ 111 : Phase E

Let us straight away get into the focus of this questions and see the situation through which the Enterprise Architect is supposed to pick up the best choice. We do not want to take the time of the Readers into other descriptions which rarely add value to the way answer is arrived for the question.

The Architectural Project started in Vision Phase and has successfully completed all iterations and all versions under Phase B, C and D, through what is popularly called BDAT (Business, Data, Application and Technology).

Which could be the best answer that suggests the steps needed well before arriving at final Migration and Development decision.

A. The EA would examine the architecture work as available as of date. EA will ensue that the Architectural work is complete as per scope and the descriptions and diagrams and other artifacts are accurate and that they are addressing all known gaps. EA will have to very specifically look into all functional requirements as also all integration requirements. EA has to further ensure that all dependencies are understood and are well documented. Next task would be to create the necessary and additional artifacts in the form of major work packages and transition architectures. At this stage the project charters for the recommended projects are also prepared.

B. The EA would examine the architecture work as available as of date. EA will prioritize projects to transition the organization from the current architecture to target architecture. This will include a business value for each project, the resources required and the intended timing. EA would then validate the prioritizations with the board particularly looking at cost benefits and risks. Finally, EA would generate the Architecture Implementation Roadmap and document lessons learned.

C. EA would assess the requirements of the organization particularly those requirements describing the functions required and information flows within the architecture. EA would then ask the Team to produce artifacts that describe the recommended projects. This would also include Gap Analysis based artifacts to move current architecture to the recommended target architectures. EA would present recommendations to the board for agreement at the end of every Phase. Once this is done, EA would ask the architects to start developing the code.

D. EA would look at the corporate culture and attitude to change, understanding the constraints such skill sets. EA will determine Business Constraints for Implementation. EA will ensue that the Architectural work is complete as per scope and the descriptions and diagrams and other artifacts are accurate and that they are addressing all known gaps. EA will have to very specifically look into all functional requirements as also all integration requirements. EA to review Consolidated Requirements Across Related Business Functions. EA has to further ensure that all dependencies are understood and are well documented. EA will review and ensure the Readiness and Risk for Business Transformation. Next task would be to create the necessary and additional artifacts in the form of major work packages and transition architectures. At this stage the project charters for the recommended projects are also prepared.

Proceeding to tackle the question and getting full five marks:

As you read the question, note the following points:

Currently in : Architectural Project started in Vision Phase and has successfully completed all iterations and all versions under Phase B, C and D

To do : The steps needed **well before arriving at final Migration and Development** decision

(So, not Phase F. But one before that)

How should we approach this Scenario based question ?

We need to identify the portion of TOGAF® documentation (available online during Level 2 Exam) so that we can quickly go to that portion and focus only on that. Not more than half a minute to be spent on this.

See the phrase : "steps needed well before arriving at final Migration and Development decision". This is the first clue that question is about Phase E, since that is the Phase that is just before Phase F : Migration Planning.

Note that Phase E : Opportunities and Solutions is "initial Migration Planning while Phase F is "final" Migration Planning.

Further clue is from the four answer choices which keep mentioning the points that are in the steps of Phase E.

Let us open 9.3 Steps[15] **(of Phase E: Opportunities & Solutions)**

9. Phase E: Opportunities & Solutions

Chapter Contents: 9.1 Objectives | 9.2 Inputs | 9.3 Steps | 9.4 Outputs | 9.5 Approach

These are :

- 9.3.1 Determine / Confirm Key Corporate Change Attributes
- 9.3.2 Determine Business Constraints for Implementation
- 9.3.3 Review and Consolidate Gap Analysis Results from Phases B to D
- 9.3.4 Review Consolidated Requirements Across Related Business Functions
- 9.3.5 Consolidate and Reconcile Interoperability Requirements
- 9.3.6 Refine and Validate Dependencies
- 9.3.7 Confirm Readiness and Risk for Business Transformation
- 9.3.8 Formulate Implementation and Migration Strategy
- 9.3.9 Identify and Group Major Work Packages
- 9.3.10 Identify Transition Architectures
- 9.3.11 Create the Architecture Roadmap & Implementation and Migration Plan

All we have to do is to look at the steps from online documentation and compare them with each of the four answers. Points in **regular bold** are positive and ones in *italics bold* are negative, in the following detailing. The **regular bold** portions indicate conformance with the step / point. If you see any portion shown in *italics bold*, it is an indication that

15. https://pubs.opengroup.org/togaf-standard/adm/chap09.html#tag_09_03

the answer has gone against the step / point or has missed it.

Looking at answer choice A:

Examining the architecture for completion and accurate and on addressing any gaps

9.3.3 Review and Consolidate Gap Analysis Results from Phases B to D

Consolidate and integrate the gap analysis results from the Business, Information Systems, and Technology Architectures (created in Phases B to D) and assess their implications with respect to potential solutions and inter-dependencies

Looking at functional and integration requirements

9.3.5 Consolidate and Reconcile Interoperability Requirements

Consolidate the interoperability requirements identified in previous phases

Ensuring that all dependencies are understood and documented

9.3.6 Refine and Validate Dependencies

Refine the initial dependencies, ensuring that any constraints on the Implementation and Migration Plans are identified

Create major work packages and transition architectures and the project charters

9.3.9 Identify and Group Major Work Packages

Key stakeholders, planners, and the Enterprise Architects should assess the missing business capabilities identified in the Architecture Vision and Target Architecture

Using the Consolidated Gaps, Solutions, and Dependencies matrix together with the Implementation Factor Assessment and Deduction matrix, logically group the various activities into work packages

But points missed out include:

Key Corporate Change Attributes

Business Constraints for Implementation

Consolidated Requirements Across Related Business Functions

Readiness and Risk for Business Transformation

Implementation and Migration Strategy

Identifying Transition Architectures (Very important point)

Observation : Points mentioned are fine, but missed points include important ones too

Looking at answer choice B:

The EA would examine the architecture work as available as of date. True. But the examination of Consolidated Gap Analysis Results from Phases B to D is more important and is a specific point that is missing here

EA will prioritize projects to transition the organization from the current architecture to target architecture. Partly correct. See 9.3.10 below

9.3.10 Identify Transition Architectures : Development of Transition Architectures must be based upon the preferred implementation approach, the Consolidated Gaps, Solutions, and Dependencies matrix, the listing of projects and portfolios, as well as the enterprise's capacity for creating and absorbing change

This will include a business value for each project, the resources required and the intended timing. These are steps in Phase F whereas this question is on a Phase prior to that

EA would then validate the prioritizations with the board particularly looking at cost benefits and risks. These are steps in Phase F and Board is not directly involved in these

Finally, EA would generate the Architecture Implementation Roadmap and document lessons learned. These are steps in Phase F

But points missed out include:

Key Corporate Change Attributes

Business Constraints for Implementation

Consolidated Requirements Across Related Business Functions

Readiness and Risk for Business Transformation

Implementation and Migration Strategy

Observation : Steps mentioned are more for Phase F. Only a partly correct answer seen here. Missed points

Looking at answer choice C:

EA would assess the requirements of the organization particularly those requirements describing the functions required and information flows within the architecture. EA would then ask the Team to produce artifacts that describe the recommended projects. This would also include Gap Analysis based artifacts to move current architecture to the recommended target architectures. Every point here is performed in Phases B to D while the present question is on Phase E

EA would present recommendations to the board for agreement at the end of every Phase. Not True. Board is brought

into picture only for a final approval

Once this is done, EA would ask the architects to start developing the code. Not True. As per TOGAF®, it is the PMO – Project Management Office which will look into actual code development issues, with Architects producing the design only

Observation : Every point is wrong

Looking at answer choice D:

EA would look at the corporate culture and attitude to change, understanding the constraints such skill sets. EA will determine Business Constraints for Implementation. EA will ensue that the Architectural work is complete as per scope and the descriptions and diagrams and other artifacts are accurate and that they are addressing all known gaps. EA will have to very specifically look into all functional requirements as also all integration requirements. EA to review Consolidated Requirements Across Related Business Functions. EA has to further ensure that all dependencies are understood and are well documented. EA will review and ensure the Readiness and Risk for Business Transformation. Next task would be to create the necessary and additional artifacts in the form of major work packages and transition architectures. At this stage the project charters for the recommended projects are also prepared

Why is every point marked as positive ? Because it matches the following:

- **9.3.1 Determine / Confirm Key Corporate Change Attributes**
- **9.3.2 Determine Business Constraints for Implementation**
- **9.3.3 Review and Consolidate Gap Analysis Results from Phases B to D**
- **9.3.4 Review Consolidated Requirements Across Related Business Functions**
- **9.3.5 Consolidate and Reconcile Interoperability Requirements**
- **0.3.6 Refine and Validate Dependencies**
- **9.3.7 Confirm Readiness and Risk for Business Transformation**
- **9.3.8 Formulate Implementation and Migration Strategy**
- **9.3.9 Identify and Group Major Work Packages**
- **9.3.10 Identify Transition Architectures**
- **9.3.11 Create the Architecture Roadmap & Implementation and Migration Plan**

Observation : Matches Phase E steps in full

Conclusion and Answer:

Go through all four Observations.

The answer will be:

Best answer : D

Every point therein is correct and matches TOGAF® documentation for steps in Phase E.

A : Second best answer.

Points answered are fine, but a few missing points.

B : Third best answer.

Only partly correct answer found.

C : This is a distractor; every point is out of the situations for the question.

SQ 112 : Phase F

IWillDo Inc is an organisation that offers Personal Assistant activities. The organisation is active worldwide and offers services to small and medium sized businesses.

They have a full Enterprise Architecture capability with TOGAF®, with role, processes, governance and ADM implemented. They have identified the first project to run under TOGAF® : Birthday Gift Services. It will be a new business service meant to take care of sending birthday presents to their customer's beloved. This service includes new processes, new information systems and a new infrastructure to be rolled out.

At this moment, the architecture development has reached the migration and planning phase. Due to the large customer base it has been decided that the risk of failure is high, that means it is not wise to expose all the customers at once to this new service. The CEO mentioned in the beginning of the architecture project that he wants to see a clear way on how this is handled.

The Consultant is supporting the organization in their EA practice. You are one of our consultants and you have been asked how to handle the Migration Planning Phase. This plan will then be presented to the CEO. Based on TOGAF®, which of the answers describe the best steps to take?

A. The CEO has a clear concern which must be addressed during the Migration Planning phase. You, together with the project leader make a breakdown of work packages. You also make sure that the project management approach aligns with the Architecture Development process. You decide to roll out the new service by breaking it down in geographic regions and customer size. For each work package you assign business value and clearly define the ROI, CSFs and Measure of Effectiveness. When this is done you make a more detailed plan on resource requirements, timing and you make a risk validation. Now you have detailed the migration-plan that is ready to give the CEO a more measurable and controllable way to deliver the service. Each work package is measurable while being delivered on value and success factors.

B. The CEO has defined a clear stakeholder concern; you select the proper viewpoint from the Continuum library and present the view. During the viewpoint selection process you take a major focus on the business architecture, this especially since we are delivering a new service. The business-service and function catalogs are the most applicable for this task and so you select them. You present the view to the CEO and show the relationships with all the organisational units and other function areas. This should convince the CEO that all relationships are clear and that the implementation by the project team will lead to a controllable process.

C. The CEO has a genuine concern. However, this is not something to worry about during the Migration Planning Phase. It needs to be addressed to the Project leader who is responsible for implementing of the project, who in turn can take up the point and place it into the project brief. During architecture reviews we focus in this Phase only on what the status is and how to mitigate the risk. The architecture contract will also contain some focus on this risk and the project will take care of this situation. During the project implementation, the architecture review process will make sure that the implementation is in accordance with the specification. This advice should now satisfy the CEO.

D. During the Migration Planning Phase, you perform the consolidated gap analysis and it will make sure that this gap will come up. You run a business transformation readiness assessment to identify gaps for implementation. The issues can be managed with risk management to make sure the residual risk is at the level that the CEO accepts. You identify the transition architectures and from that the project manager can start the migration-planning.

Proceeding to tackle the question and getting full five marks:

As you read the question, note the following points:

Issues in focus : Identified that the first project to run under TOGAF®. Service includes new processes, new information systems and a new infrastructure to be rolled out. Risk of failure is high, not wise to expose all the customers at once to this new service

To do : Best steps to be taken to handle the Migration Planning Phase

How should we approach this Scenario based question?

We need to identify the portion of TOGAF® documentation (available online during Level 2 Exam) so that we can quickly go to that portion and focus only on that. Not more than half a minute to be spent on this.

Let us open **Chapter 10 : Phase F: Migration Planning**[16]. And move to 10.3 Steps.

10. Phase F: Migration Planning

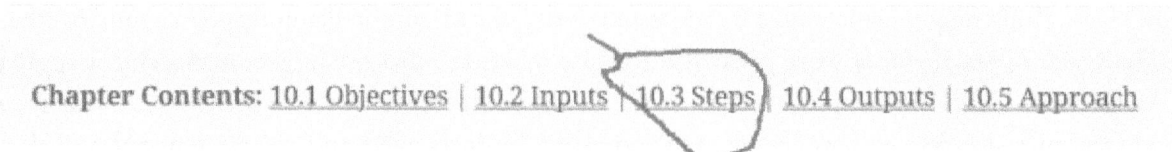

Chapter Contents: 10.1 Objectives | 10.2 Inputs | 10.3 Steps | 10.4 Outputs | 10.5 Approach

All we have to do is to look at the steps from online documentation and compare them with each of the four answers. Points in **regular bold** are positive and ones in *italics bold* are negative, in the following detailing. The **regular bold** portions indicate conformance with the step / point. If you see any portion shown in *italics bold*, it is an indication that the answer has gone against the step / point or has missed it.

Looking at answer choice A:

The CEO has a clear concern which must be addressed during the Migration Planning Phase

You, together with the project leader make a breakdown of work packages. You decide to roll out the new service by breaking it down in geographic regions and customer size

10.4 Outputs[17]

— Project and portfolio breakdown of the implementation:

— Allocation of work packages to project and portfolio

You also make sure that the project management approach aligns with the Architecture Development process

---

16. **https://pubs.opengroup.org/togaf-standard/adm/chap10.html**

17. https://pubs.opengroup.org/togaf-standard/adm/chap10.html#tag_10_04

: 10.3.1 Confirm Management Framework Interactions for the Implementation and Migration Plan : Project/ Portfolio Management that co-ordinates, designs, and builds the business systems that deliver the concrete business outcomes

For each work package you assign business value and clearly define the ROI, CSFs and Measure of Effectiveness : See 10.3.2 Assign a Business Value to Each Work Package and find out how ROI and other measures are covered here

When this is done you make a more detailed plan on resource requirements, timing and you make a risk validation : 10.3.3 Estimate Resource Requirements, Project Timings, and Availability/Delivery Vehicle. This step determines the required resources and times for each project and their increments and provides the initial cost estimates

Risks should then be assigned to the projects and project increments by aggregating risks identified in the Consolidated Gaps, Solutions, and Dependencies Matrix : 10.3.2 : Risks should then be assigned to the projects and project increments by aggregating risks identified in the Consolidated Gaps, Solutions, and Dependencies Matrix (from Phase E).

Now you have detailed the migration-plan that is ready to give the CEO a more measurable and controllable way to deliver the service. Each work package is measurable while being delivered on value and success factors : 10.3.5 Confirm Architecture Roadmap and Update Architecture Definition Document: .. taking into consideration the increments in business value and capability and other factors, such as risk

Observation : All are very relevant points, mapping to Chapter 10. Phase F: Migration Planning

Looking at answer choice B:

The CEO has defined a clear stakeholder concern; *you select the proper viewpoint from the Continuum library and present the view*. Not something done at this stage. Has TOGAF® mentioned any Viewpoints in Phase F?

During the viewpoint selection process you take a major focus on the business architecture, this especially since we are delivering a new service. Irrelevant in Phase F

The business-service and function catalogs are the most applicable for this task and so you select them. Not in Phase F

You present the risk view to the CEO and show the relationships with all the organisational units and other function areas. This should convince the CEO that all relationships are clear and that the implementation by the project team will lead to a controllable process. Step partly correct, but it goes to the Board, not CEO

10.3.4 : Formally review the risk assessment and revise it as necessary ensuring that there is a full understanding of the residual risk associated with the prioritization and the projected funding line. The review is done at this stage, but goes to the Board afterwards

Observation : Answers are way out, except being part correct in one last point

Looking at answer choice C:

The CEO has a genuine concern. However, this is not something to worry about during the Migration Planning Phase. Concerns of this nature has to be addressed

It needs to be addressed to the Project leader who is responsible for implementing of the project, who in turn can take up the point and place it into the project brief. Wrong. EA should address this

During architecture reviews we focus in this Phase only on what the status is and how to mitigate the risk. Review is at every Phase, all the more in Phase E & F, when it comes to solutions and risk

The architecture contract will also contain some focus this risk and the project will take care of this situation. During the project implementation, the architecture review process will make sure that the implementation is in accordance with the specification. This advice should now satisfy the CEO. Architecture Contact is made at Phase G and if at all prepared earlier, Phase F may only prepare a draft of it. Project Management alone cannot handle this risk

Observation : All points are wrong

Looking at answer choice D:

During the Migration Planning Phase, you perform the consolidated gap analysis and it will make sure that this gap will come up. This analysis is done in Phase E

You run a business transformation readiness assessment to identify gaps for implementation. Also done in Phase E

The issues can be managed with risk management to make sure the residual risk is at the level that the CEO accepts

You identify the transition architectures and from that the project manager can start the migration-planning. **Identified at Phase E. Migration Plan conducted by EA**

You may recommend another leaner cycle of ADM, taking the complexity of the situation at hand

10.3.7 : Depending upon the level of the Target Architecture and Implementation and Migration Plan it may be necessary to iterate another ADM cycle at a lower level of detail

Observation : More acceptable points compared to the previous answer choice

Conclusion and Answer:

Go through all four Observations.

The answer will be:

Best answer : A

The only answer that fits in the steps of Phase F to an acceptable level.

D : Second best answer. More positive points and less of negative points.

B : Third best answer. Some points only are relevant.

C : This is a distractor; is the worst answer for obvious reasons.

SQ 113 : Implementation Governance

Note that this is an ADM Phase whereas Architectural Governance is a topic that covers the whole of the EA process. There is some commonality in both.

(Details about the industry and such other statistics, which usually appear in these questions is skipped here. Such descriptions do not add much value in finding the answer, or even in understanding the question)

In this ADM cycle, a portfolio of projects has been taken up. For these the detailed implementation and migration plan is completed. We are just about to start the Implementation Governance.

The concern of stakeholders, especially Top Management is that core and critical risks are not addressed and perhaps are not fully identified.

Come up with your best answer for approaching this situation, noting that Program Management Office will be carrying out actual implementation (coding testing and migration from existing systems to new systems).

A. You will have to work out the actual implementation program and the way it transits from the Architecture and Design to the development platform. This will be done through an Architecture Contract. This will help the projects to be steered through a series of transitions while they continue to deliver business value. You work out the mechanism conduct risk management reviews, during and after the Phase G operations. You are confident that any of the risk situations can be tackled after the project is complete

B. You start with the approval of the Implementation and Migration Plan. You do this by confirming Scope and Priorities for Deployment with Development Management. You indicate to PMO the intention of performing Enterprise Architecture Compliance Reviews. You also conduct post-implementation reviews and then publish reviews and close projects. You decide that the PMO should enable early realization of business value and benefits, and to minimize the risk in the transformation and migration program, the favored approach is to deploy the Target Architecture as a series of transitions. Each transition represents an incremental step towards the target, and each delivers business benefit in its own right

C. You inform the Architecture Board the intention of initiating an Architecture Compliance Review (ACR) for the architecture project. The ACR, to be detailed by you, will review the question if the target architecture responds to the needs of the enterprise. It will look into issues of risks where identified and mitigated. You are ready to start yet another ADM iteration for specific needs, in case risks that are identified earlier are not mitigated as found in the review. All these will be reflected in the Architecture Contract that you draw up with the Development Team and also the one with the Business Stakeholders. Still you will have a good oversight and conduct periodic informal review on architectural points as the implementation projects progress.

D. You inform the Architecture Board the intention of initiating an Architecture Compliance Review (ACR) for the architecture project. The ACR, to be detailed by you, will review the question if the target architecture responds to the needs of the enterprise. It will look into issues of risks where identified and mitigated. You will only look at quick-fix in case risks that are identified by us are not mitigated as found in the review. All these will be reflected in the Architecture Contract that you draw up with he Development Team and also the one with the Business Stakeholders. Still you will have a good oversight and conduct periodic informal review on architectural points as the implementation projects progress.

Proceeding to tackle the question and getting full five marks:

As you read the question, note the following points:

Issues in focus : The concern of stakeholders, especially Top Management is that core and critical risks are not addressed and perhaps are not fully identified.

Aims : Provide a good risk mitigation approach, for the risks which will come up during Phase G, though other risks noticed up to Phase F would have been taken care of already.

To do : Decide the course of action

How should we approach this Scenario based question?

You need to open, in the online documentation:

11. Phase G: Implementation Governance[18]

11. Phase G: Implementation Governance

Chapter Contents: 11.1 Objectives | 11.2 Inputs | 11.3 Steps | 11.4 Outputs | 11.5 Approach

Points in **regular bold** are positive and ones in *italics bold* are negative, in the following detailing. The **regular bold** portions indicate conformance with the step / point. If you see any portion shown in *italics bold*, it is an indication that the answer has gone against the step / point or has missed it.

Looking at answer choice A:

You will have to work out the actual implementation program and the way it transits from the Architecture and Design to the development platform. This will be done through an Architecture Contract. This will help the projects to be steered through a series of transitions while they continue to deliver business value. You emphasize on a mechanism conduct risk management reviews, during and after the Phase G operations. You are confident that any of the risk situations can be tackled after the project is complete

All these are points connected to Phase G. But none of them are specific in addressing eh concern raised. It suggests that risks management reviews are needed but does not say how to proceed towards that same

Observation : Suggestion moves us asway from the reality on risk mitigation

---

Looking at answer choice B:

You start with the approval of the Implementation and Migration Plan. You do this by confirming Scope and Priorities for Deployment with Development Management. Very general points for Phase G. Not for the concern at hand

You indicate to PMO the intention of performing Enterprise Architecture Compliance Reviews. You also conduct post-implementation reviews and then publish reviews and close projects. Right direction, but without details

You decide that the PMO should enable early realization of business value and benefits, and to minimize the risk in the transformation and migration program, the favored approach is to deploy the Target Architecture as a series of transitions. Each transition represents an incremental step towards the target, and each delivers business benefit in its own right. Points are fine for Phase G, but not for the concern that needs addressing

Observation : Only some points make sense

Looking at answer choice C:

You inform the Architecture Board the intention of initiating an Architecture Compliance Review (ACR) for the architecture project. The ACR, to be detailed by you, will review the question if the target architecture responds to the needs of the enterprise. It will look into issues of risks where identified and mitigated. You are ready to start yet another ADM iteration for specific needs, in case risks that are identified earlier are not mitigated as found in the review. All these will be reflected in the Architecture Contract that you draw up with the Development Team and also the one with the Business Stakeholders. Still you will have a good oversight and conduct periodic informal review on architectural points as the implementation projects progress

Observation : All are very relevant and are focussed towards addressing the concern raised

Looking at answer choice D:

You inform the Architecture Board the intention of initiating an Architecture Compliance Review (ACR) for the architecture project. The ACR, to be detailed by you, will review the question if the target architecture responds to the needs of the enterprise. It will look into issues of risks where identified and mitigated

You will only look at quick-fix in case risks that are identified by us are not mitigated as found in the review

All these will be reflected in the Architecture Contract that you draw up with the Development Team and also the one with the Business Stakeholders. Still you will have a good oversight and conduct periodic informal review on architectural points as the implementation projects progress

Note that the negative potion above is not an ideal way to look at the risk areas once they are noticed

Observation : Most points make sense, but not all

Conclusion and Answer:

Go through all four Observations.

The answer will be:

Best answer : C

All points are toward risk addressed.

D : Second best answer. More positive points and less of negative points.

B : Third best answer. Some points only are relevant.

A : This is a distractor; is the worst answer for obvious reasons.

SQ 114 : Compliance Review

Smart Inc. is a company that delivers 3D printing facilities. Customers can create 3D models themselves and send their designs up to this enterprise and they will print the plastic models.

Currently a project is running to implement a new customer complaint service. New information systems are needed to offer better services online and integration with a cloud services delivering CRM and the company's own system is also needed.

The Architecture Board has concerns about the way the integration takes place between the cloud provider and their own CRM database. The board is especially concerned about additional customer information being shared, which was not part of the scope.

You, as an EA, are part of the Architecture Board and are asked to take proper measures about it. Based on TOGAF®, what would be the best approach ?

A. Your advice is to run an architecture compliance review process. You ask the lead architect to take the review co-ordinator role. You specifically ask a review for the whole scope of the project. This process will investigate what the project compliance is in relation to the architecture design. A finding of the review is that there is indeed more information shared with the cloud solution than was designed in the ADD. However, all that was designed is in. You bring this back to the board by stating that the status of the compliance is : conformant. There is the risk that this information does not belong to the cloud service and would violate privacy rules.

B. Your advice is to ask the lead architect to take the ADD and check what is inside; if it does not mention the additional information to be delivered to the cloud provider then there is no issue. You bring this information back to the board. The architect can then define a gap that should be addressed inside the target architecture.

C. You propose that the lead architect should wait for project to end and then do a Lesson Learnt session after. That should be enough to cover this subject, the main concern is that the solution will work. Doing more can never harm the system in the first place.

D. You provide advice the board to run an architecture compliance review process. They could ask the information manager who is involved in the project to take the review co-ordinator role. You specifically ask a review for the integration part to limit the scope. This process will investigate what the project compliance is in relation to the architecture design. Also interview the project principals. As a result of the review you find out that there is indeed more information shared with the cloud solution than was designed in the ADD. However, all that was designed is in. You bring this back to the board by stating that the status of the compliance is : conformant. There is the risk that this information does not belong in the cloud service and would violate privacy rules. You provide a recommendation to resolve and/or proceed with this matter.

Proceeding to tackle the question and getting full five marks:

As you read the question, note the following points:

Issues in focus : A project is running to implement a new customer complaint service

Concerns about the way the integration takes place between the cloud provider and their own CRM database

To do : Addressing the concerns, by following process of Compliance Review properly

(Note : ADD is Architecture Definition Document)

How should we approach this Scenario based question?

We need to identify the portion of TOGAF® documentation (available online during Level 2 Exam) so that we can quickly go to that portion and focus only on that. Not more than half a minute to be spent on this.

See : Chapter 6 : Architecture Compliance[19]

Enterprise Architecture Capability and Governance
6. Architecture Compliance

Focus on : 6.4.3 Steps[20]

These are :

Request ...

Identify ..

Identify ...

Determine ....

Tailor ..

Schedule ..

Interview ..

Analyze ... - Review against ... Identify ....

Determine ...

Prepare ...

Present ... - To Architecture Board

All we have to do is to look at the steps from online documentation and compare them with each of the four answers. Points in **regular bold** are positive and ones in *italics bold* are negative, in the following detailing. The **regular bold** portions indicate conformance with the step / point. If you see any portion shown in *italics bold*, it is an indication that the answer has gone against the step / point or has missed it.

---

19. https://pubs.opengroup.org/togaf-standard/ea-capability-and-governance/chap06.html

20. https://pubs.opengroup.org/togaf-standard/ea-capability-and-governance/chap06.html#tag_06_04_03

Looking at answer choice A:

Your advice is to run an architecture compliance review process : Request architecture review

You ask the lead architect to take the review co-ordinator role : Identify responsible part of organization and relevant project principals. Role of Architecture Review Co-ordinator *(TOGAF® suggests a separate Review co-ordinator role, different from Lead Architect).* Next step is : Identify Lead Enterprise Architect and other architects

You specifically ask a review for the whole scope of the project : Determine scope of review – Identify which other business units/departments are involved. Understand where the system fits in the corporate architecture framework

This process will investigate what the project compliance is in relation to the architecture design : Tailor checklists

Not covered : Interview project principals

A finding of the review is that there is indeed more information shared with the cloud **solution than was designed in the ADD. However, all that was designed is in :** Analyze completed checklists - Review against corporate standards. Identify and resolve issues

You bring this back to the board by stating that the status of the compliance is : conformant : Determine recommendations

There is the risk that this information does not belong to the cloud service and would violate privacy rules : Prepare Architecture review report; Present review findings - To Architecture Board

Observation : Couple of wrong or missing points

Looking at answer choice B:

Your advice is to ask the lead architect to take the ADD and check what is inside; if it does not mention the additional information to be delivered to the cloud provider then there is no issue. You bring this information back to the board. The architect can then define a gap that should be addressed inside the target architecture

Review process is distorted in this answer. But at least some kind of re-check is suggested

Observation : recheck is an acceptable point

Looking at answer choice C:

You propose that the lead architect should wait for project to end and then do a Lesson Learnt session after. That

should be enough to cover this subject, the main concern is that the solution will work. Doing more can never harm the system in the first place

Review process is not at all suggested

Observation : Totally distorted approach

Looking at answer choice D:

You provide advice the board to run an architecture compliance review process. They could ask the information manager who is involved in the project to take the review co-ordinator role. You specifically ask a review for the integration part to limit the scope. This process will investigate what the project compliance is in relation to the architecture design. Also interview the project principals. As a result of the review you find out that there is indeed more information shared with the cloud solution than was designed in the ADD. However, all that was designed is in. You bring this back to the board by stating that the status of the compliance is : conformant. There is the risk that this information does not belong in the cloud service and would violate privacy rules. You provide a recommendation to resolve and/or proceed with this matter

Why all **positive** ? See point by point discussion below:

You advice the board to run an architecture compliance review process : Request architecture review

They could ask the information manager who is involved in the project to take the review co-ordinator role : Identify responsible part of organization and relevant project principals. Role of Architecture Review Co-ordinator. Identify Lead Enterprise Architect and other architects

You specifically ask a review for the integration part to limit the scope : Determine scope of review – Identify which other business units/departments are involved. Understand where the system fits in the corporate architecture framework

This process will investigate what the project compliance is in relation to the architecture design : Tailor checklists

Interview project principals : As Step 7

As a result of the review you find out that there is indeed more information shared with the cloud solution than was designed in the ADD. However, all that was designed is in : Analyze completed checklists - Review against corporate standards. Identify and resolve issues

You bring this back to the board by stating that the status of the compliance is : conformant : Determine recommendations

You provide a recommendation to resolve and/or proceed with this matter : Also part of Determine recommendations

There is the risk that this information does not belong in the cloud service and would violate privacy rules :

Prepare Architecture review report; Present review findings - To Architecture Board

Observation : Everything stated is fine and covers the required steps for the Compliance Review

Conclusion and Answer:

Go through all four Observations.

The answer will be:

Best answer : D

Every point therein is correct and is complete.

A : Second best answer.

Though not a "best answer" in that sense, among the choices this ranks second.

B : Third best answer.

Though not a "best answer" in that sense, among the choices this ranks next.

C : This is a distractor; Every point is wrong.

About the various Book Series available from the same Author :

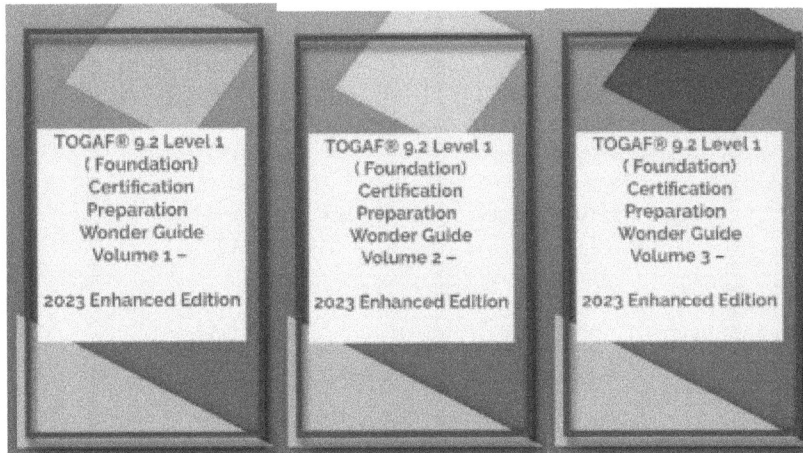

The three volumes together make up for your preparation for Level 1 Exam – TOGAF® 9.2

This 9.2 Certification is kept open even as TOGAF 10 Certification has started.

Might remain so for quite a few months ahead

TOGAF® 9.2 Level 2

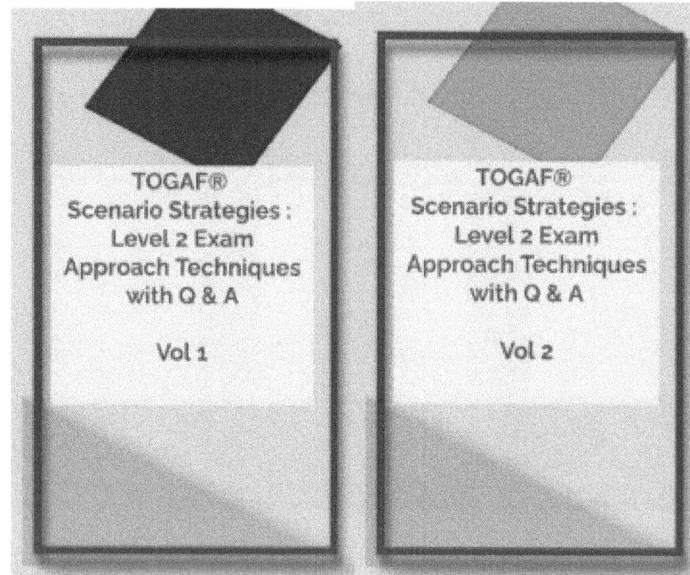

The two volumes together makes up for your preparation for Level 2 Exam – TOGAF® 9.2

Ideally **TOGAF® 10** can be approached with a One hour exam,

if you possess TOGAF® 9.2 or TOGAF® 9.1 Certification

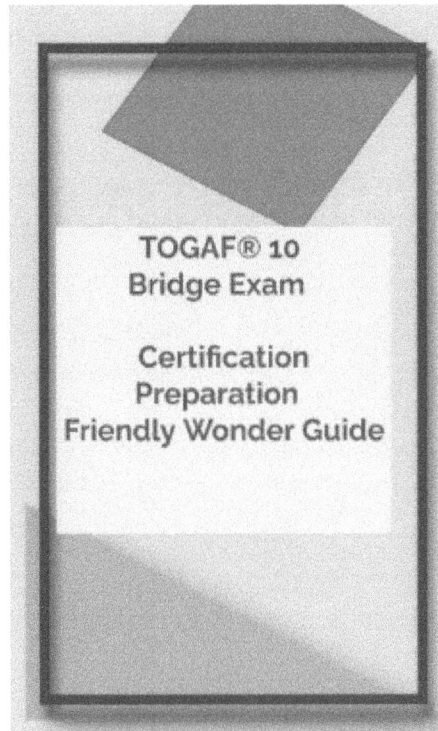

Our Book which can steer you to **TOGAF® 10** through the Bridge Exam

And for those who want to take TOGAF® 10 fresh, our emerging Book Series happen to be :

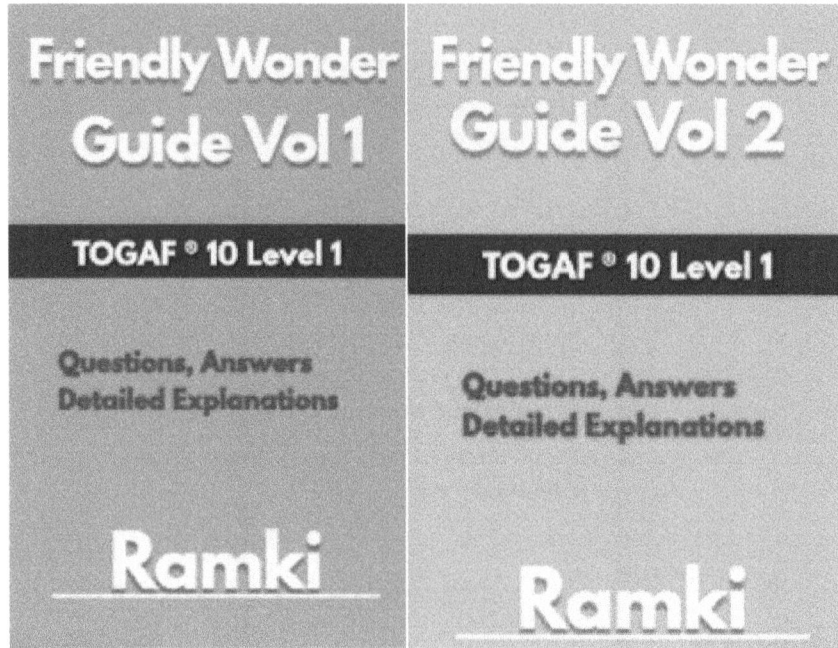

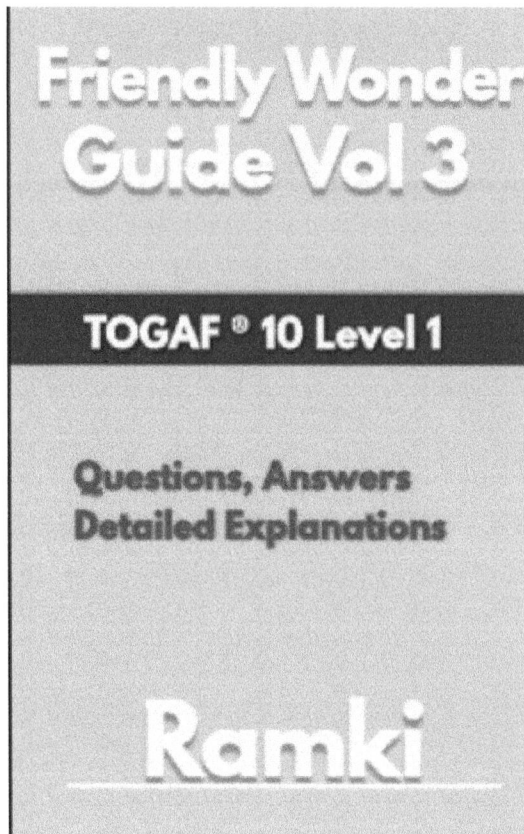

As also Volumes on Level 2 tilted as Scenario Strategies for TOGAF® 10 Exam

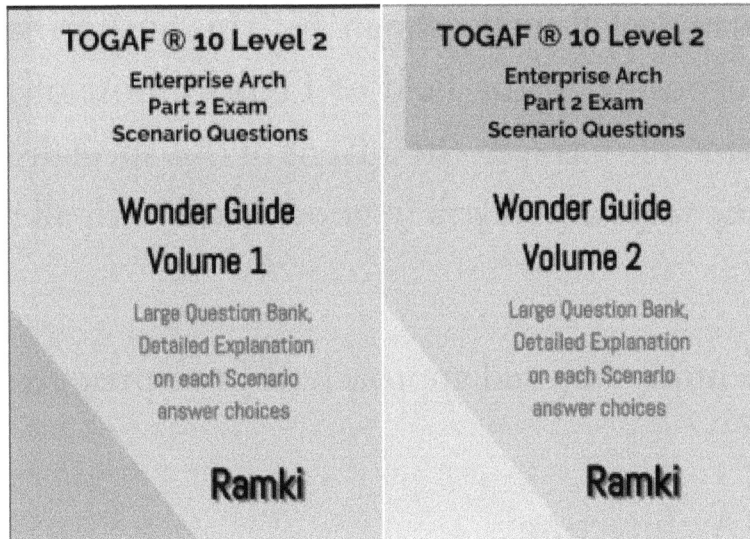

This Book is one among the two

And to be really practical and ready with TOGAF Competence :

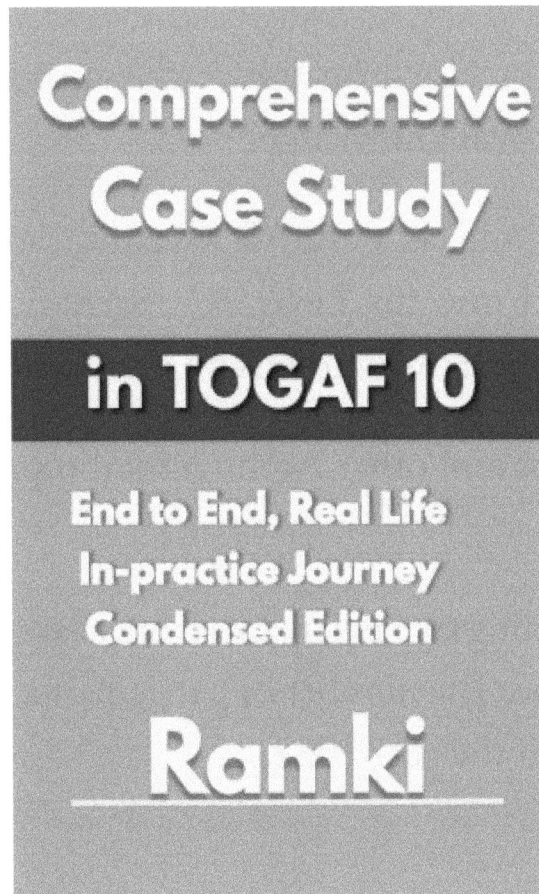

Author & Expert Faculty : **Ramakrishnan N (Ramki)**

Ramki is the pen name of Ramakrishnan N. This author has nearly 50 years of experience and exposure in the field of IT, and most of it is attributed to Software Architecture. He has seen the advent of this specialist field of Software Architecture over the years and is still in good touch with all modern evolution of the same.

TOGAF® 10 places more focussed approach of Enterprise Architecture getting into areas such as :

- Microservice Architecture
- Digital Enterprise and Digital Technology Adoption : Digital Business Reference Model (DBRM)
- Information Mapping and Organization Mapping
- Customer Master Data Management (C-MDM)
- TOGAF® ADM using Agile Sprints

These happen to be the precise areas where the author has equipped himself with practical and conceptual knowledge.

Books of same author, Ramki, as TOGAF® Certification Wonder Books (three volumes for Level 1 and one for Level 2 – Scenario Strategies) have been admired and being purchased by hundreds on a day to day basis.

Books on Design Patterns and other Architectural topics are also to the credit of this author.

He has also provided training to participants from a large number of Enterprises spanning all over the globe. The number of participants to his TOGAF® courses alone is close to 2000 as of the year 2022.

Reachable through: mramkiz@gmail.com

Don't miss out!

Visit the website below and you can sign up to receive emails whenever Ramki publishes a new book. There's no charge and no obligation.

https://books2read.com/r/B-A-AHMW-IFMKC

BOOKS 2 READ

Connecting independent readers to independent writers.

9 798223 359708